PNЯ251

VOLUME 46   NUMBER 3   JANUARY – FEBRUARY 2020

--------- R E P O R T S ---------   --------- R E V I E W S ---------

--------- P O E M S & F E A T U R E S ---------

Editorial

ONCE UPON A TIME *PN Review* had more than 300 library subscribers in the UK. Today, world-wide, it has 149 institutional subscribers, a term that embraces libraries, arts councils and other institutions. Our subscriber list has more than trebled, but our UK library subscribers are few. We cannot even boast a full flush of Russell Group universities. As for civic libraries, the number is exiguous. Yet libraries, one might have assumed, should be the core of any serious periodical's subscriber list, its way of reaching new readers and writers from all walks of life.

Sometimes a key library writes to announce that it intends to discontinue its subscription. It needs to be cajoled into accepting a gratis extra year. Even so, the cost of binding issues into volumes for long-term shelving seems to be a chief bugbear among the older libraries. There is also the cost of cataloguing, the issue of space, and the fact that, compared with a new computer station or a best-selling novel, a literary journal has relatively few users.

But in library terms, relatively few people access most of the print material held. It is held because some people *do* access it. The library is, or was, less a populist than a democratic space, where readers with a variety of special interests can, or could, find texts important to them. Such readers may themselves not have constituted a significant statistical percentage of overall library users, but they were nonetheless important. Many, let down by the library service, have lost the habit. The Internet is not an adequate substitute, but it's all some of them have, unless their resources extend to a personal library or an individual subscription.

One reason we had, all those years ago, so many UK library subscribers is that the Arts Council of Great Britain's policy for its chosen journals was to provide subscriptions to libraries gratis, on the grounds that the best way to support readers, writers, libraries and magazines was to facilitate the end user's access. Six or seven journals were offered, and libraries could opt in to the scheme. It was considered better to create pull than to contribute to push, to support use rather than production. What mattered in publishing new literature and critical writing was not marketing and selling but (libraries being libraries) provision.

The hope was that the libraries would, after a period of years, take over the cost of subscribing, having built up a reader base. This proved to be wishful thinking. When the scheme had run its course, not all, not many, of the libraries that had benefited found budget to continue subscribing. Major periodical beneficiaries – the *New Review*, for example – suffered and ceased publication. Others adapted as best they could to the new order, which was the old order restored. Subsidy, where it survived, reverted to the earlier pattern of support for production.

The much-publicised crisis in our library culture often assumes that civic and institutional libraries have not really changed much in purpose or function over the years. Outrage was expressed when Manchester Central Library was refurbished and disposed of thousands of books, replacing book space with computer terminals, social and performance areas to draw in a public that had not previously felt at ease in the hushed space where people went to read and find out what was old and new. Despite the commendable interests of wider public engagement, some critics and some erstwhile readers felt libraries were losing sight of their original, devoted and even dependent constituencies. Their buying policies no longer privileged the various minorities (and here I do not mean ethnic or social minorities but those groups with minority interests in, for example, steam engines, local history, origami, poetry) for which the library was an irreplaceable resource.

The argument is that the Internet provides, largely free of charge, much that before required non-digital skills to access. Manchester Central Library has more users than it did before, but probably not more readers. Certainly its periodical resources are depleted in comparison to what they were. And *PN Review*, whose offices are nearby and whose contributors include many people from Manchester's communities, is no longer to be found on its shelves.

Simon Armitage is making libraries one of the causes he intends to support during his laureateship, scheduling a 'ten-year library tour'. He will spend a week every spring touring libraries because 'the very existence of the library system is under threat'. I expect that as he visits and spotlights key libraries, he will also remind them of their place in contributing to the literary health of the nation. If they are to be book and magazine places as well as computer terminals, the advocacy they require from pressure groups and powerful individuals like the poet laureate needs to be directed not only at funding bodies and the public but at the librarians themselves. A whole generation has grown up in the age of 'information culture' and has presided over, or presided during, the service's steep decline. English Library loans are down by 43% in ten years, the *Bookseller* reported in December, and 59% since the turn in the millennium.

The figures, provided by the Chartered Institute of Public Finance and Accountancy (CIPFA), are used by some Authorities to argue the obsolescence of the libraries themselves – there are more pressing priorities – and by others to drum up support for an idealised renaissance in our library culture. The indefatigable Tim Coates, quondam managing director of Waterstone's, has made it his mission to champion libraries. He can sound apocalyptic when he describes this 'terrible state' of play: repeated schemes to turn around the service have failed. With reduced buying budgets, reduced provision for readers, it is hardly surprising that loans are down. The prophecy is self-fulfilling. 'The British public library service is in a terrible state and will require major reorganisation if it is, in future, to be useful. [...] Use of the service has been falling regularly for the past twenty years, and funding has been falling for the past ten. In comparison, for example, to America and to Australia, the figures for the UK are simply dire.'

Last month, figures were released that showed a further loss of thirty-five libraries in 2018-9. Over the last ten years, 17.7% of libraries (about 800) have closed. There are now 371 libraries run by volunteers, up from 272 the previous year. Though book budgets have risen modestly, by 0.4% year on year, book prices have risen faster, and seven million fewer visits were recorded and a 4.4% fall in books issued.

The new government has been challenged to produce £250 million to 'deliver a world-class library sector,' a sum which is also intended to cover 'information and knowledge for the 21st Century'. Arts Council England has found £2 million for libraries, using its National Lottery resources. It is not yet clear what is going to be built out of the ruins of the library system. Is a new name required, one that does not foreground the printed word in the way *library* does but acknowledges that we live in an irreversibly post-Gutenberg age? In the *New Republic* (23 December), arguing that Rupi Kaur was the most important writer of the past decade, Rumaan Alam's coat-trailing article delivered some relativistic home truths of a kind that go to the heart of a contemporary value system based in a seductive, reductive technology. Is literature, is literacy, so vulnerable to, so entailed in, the populism that, in the Trump era, seems to define how we conduct not only politics but literature, the triumph of the tweet? Alam declares:

> The next generation of readers and writers views reality through a screen. Kaur, born in 1992, was 15 when the iPhone debuted. The majority of her readers have never known adulthood without that gizmo's mitigating influence. On Instagram, Kaur doesn't just share selfies and drawings; she *publishes*. Kaur's books have sold more than 3.5 million copies, an incredible number for any poet but the more remarkable when you consider that surely some percentage of her readership has never owned one of those books.

Yet one thing can be guaranteed, that in those libraries that still have some contemporary poetry on their shelves, Kaur's printed books will be available even when Geoffrey Hill's, or Anne Carson's, or Simon Armitage's, are not.

News & Notes

John Ash · *Michael Schmidt writes:* In January 2015 we had news that John Ash had returned to Manchester from Istanbul, where he had lived for many years after his earlier exile in Manhattan. He was in very poor health and had exhausted his resources. Since his return he had gradually pulled himself together (despite a series of serious hospitalisations) and had even begun, sporadically, writing poems and working on the proofs of his *Collected Poems*. He received a Royal Literature Fund pension, renewed his passport and opened a bank account. He was planning an escape from the Manchester winter and there was a glow like light at the end of a very long tunnel. But in early December his daily morning phone calls ceased, and then came news that he had died suddenly from sepsis and pneumonia.

He left Istanbul having abandoned all his possessions – books, manuscripts, records, paintings. It seemed they were irrecoverable, though in the last few weeks Carcanet has begun assembling an archive of his letters, poems and other writings in order to make the *Collected Poems* more complete and to work towards a volume of his letters. Anyone who was in regular receipt of his always handwritten missives and manuscripts knows their unparalleled value as entertainment and instruction.

Handwritten: because John did not type, did not use email or the internet, and only mastered the basics of the mobile phone when his survival depended on it. People typed for him. People did a lot for him: they supported him, they cultivated and valued him. Though he was a journalist (an extraordinary travel writer), a teacher and poet, there were times in his life when the kindness of friends and strangers was what he had to live on. He maintained a number of close, sometimes volatile friendships. John Ashbery, Christopher Middleton, Kenneth Koch and Harry Matthews were among his best-known correspondents. Friends were bound to him by his sense of humour, his enormous learning (in history, music and literature), his generosity of spirit, and his extraordinary poems. The only thing he never had much of was money.

One of his friends from his Istanbul years sent me a number of the poems he read at the poetry group with which he associated there. It consisted of young, established and striving writers, and visiting writers were welcome. This poem, his 'All-purpose Elegy', can stand as a wry selfie by the man who never mastered the camera phone, and as a taster for the poems that will follow in this and other journals, and in the *Collected*:

> O, it was here. But now it's gone!
> It is always gone or going. It was here,
> I am convinced of it, only a minute
> Or a century ago, and I already miss it.
> Gone thing, will you come back, make
> One last appearance, well-lighted like
> A sunset over a lake between terrific mountains?

Glen Cavaliero · *Kevin Gardner writes:* Glen Cavaliero, FRSL, was above all a poet – but no less a scholar, teacher, friend, and gentleman. With his death in October at the age of ninety-two, a link with the old 'Cambridge English' of Forster and Leavis was broken. Glen came to

Cambridge in 1965 to take a PhD in English; he stayed on as Fellow Commoner in St Catherine's College and remained a fixture at High Table lunch until his last illness. 'He was the best-read person I have ever met,' says Peter Scupham, 'and we used to have gentle literary teas in his rather Edwardian rooms in Cambridge.'

He wrote scholarly books on modern English literature, including studies of Forster, J.C. Powys and Charles Williams, as well as the rural tradition, the supernatural, and laughter in English fiction. He supervised many students who remember him fondly. Professor Sir Jonathan Bate recollects his Leavisite instruction: 'Among my fondest student memories are the practical criticism classes with Glen Cavaliero in which we close read dog-eared cyclostyled copies of unidentified poems. He was the most wonderfully subtle and generous teacher. And no mean poet himself.'

Glen's main legacy is surely his poetry, published in eight volumes between 1973 and 2011 by Carcanet, Tartarus and Poetry Salzburg; his collected poems, *The Flash of Weathercocks*, appeared in 2016. His work is marked by a serious religiosity – he was in Holy Orders but no longer officiated and was, as he put it, 'haunted by the presence of forsaken pieties'. In his poetry is a prevailing assurance that the shadow in which we dwell was created by light, the material world is enfolded by the numinous: 'A globe of endless flux, chasms of chaos, dried-up / lakes and flooded prairies, blinded griefs, unbridled growths / and ancient emptiness, and at its source a God impaled / on what he wills'.

Clive James · Australian-born poet Clive James's final book of poems is due to be published in 2020. He died on 24 November 2019 at the age of eighty, having been ill for a long spell (his terminal diagnosis was given a decade before his actual death). In announcing his death, Picador pointed out that he was 'the longest continuously published author on the list, with some forty titles in all. The first Picador James title was *Unreliable Memoirs*; it was an immediate bestseller and went on to sell over a million copies [...] and remained with the imprint ever since.' They quoted the *New Yorker* on his versatility: he was 'a brilliant bunch of guys': essayist, television and radio personality, memoirist, novelist and a poet with an enviable, sometimes treacherous facility. His best-selling later collections include *Sentenced to Life* and a translation of *The Divine Comedy*. His collected writings on Philip Larkin, *Somewhere Becoming Rain*, was the last book he published in his lifetime. There will doubtless be long after-tremors.

In 1992 he was made a Member of the Order of Australia and though he was so much a British media fixture there was never any doubt of his Australian roots. He was awarded an honorary doctorates from Sydney University and another by the University of East Anglia. In 2012 he was appointed CBE and, to restore the balance, in 2013 an Officer of the Order of Australia.

Amjad Nasser · The Jordanian journalist, writer and poet Amjad Nasser, known also as Yahya Numeiri al-Naimat, died in London (where he had made his home) in October 2019 at the age of sixty-four. He was one of the earliest Arabic-language explorers of the prose poem and was an important modernist voice. He was born into a Bedouin family and began writing poetry at school, where he also became a politically alert individual. He was affected by Palestinian militant movements and became an activist when he left school. In 1979 his first collection of poetry was published, with a preface by the Iraqi poet Saadi Yousef. After the siege of Beirut in 1982, he continued to work in the Palestinian media in Cyprus and from 1987 in London, specifically with the daily newspaper *Al-Quds al-Arabi*, where he wrote for and edited the culture pages. He did not enlist his poetry in the political struggle, retaining it largely as a space in which to explore forms, appropriate language, and the specifics of a life lived in a complex world. He wrote what was a new kind of love poetry in Arabic as well. His last and in some ways his most ambitious poetic work was the 2004 *Hayatun sardin mutaqatta'in ka* (*life as an intermittent narrative*). He published eight poetry volumes and was widely celebrated as one of those who forged the way for modern Arabic verse. Available to the English reader are three books drawn from his *oeuvre*, *Shepherd of Solitude: Selected Poems, 1979-2004*, translated by Khaled Mattawa (Banipal, 2009), *Land of No Rain*, translated by Jonathan Wright (A&C Black. 2014) and *Petra: The Concealed Rose*, translated by Fady Joudah (Tavern Books, 2014).

2020 Digital Transition · *Books Ireland* has announced its transition to purely digital transmission. It is primed 'to provide all the latest news, events, festivals and coverage of Irish-published, Irish-authored and Irish-interest books – but now faster than before and in ways that better suit how people stay in touch and receive their news.' After forty three years of print and latterly digital, this transition to a digital platform, supported by the Irish Arts Council, 'enables us to future-proof our ability to continue to be a leading Irish source for authoritative news for writers, readers and the book publishing sector – amplifying and supporting the work across the industry and helping this work reach new audiences.' The change is in response, the editors insist, to changes in the ways people read. They are also alert to the 'climate emergency' and are 'reducing our carbon footprint and using fewer resources in terms of paper, printing and transport.' There is the promise, which may be misplaced given the opportunities that digital provides, to 'keep the spirit of the print version and remain true to the traditions established over 43 years'. Transitions of this radical nature offer an opportunity for re-invention. Print and digital are not equivalent, any more than reading on the screen and reading on the page are equivalent experiences. Analogous, at best. There seems to be a will to enhance and broaden the offering. 'We will still have our regular reviews but we are adding new content, such as our new monthly interview series, "This Literary Life with Mary McCarthy", and providing a shared space for Irish literary-focused podcasts, as well as other new features.' *PN Review* will watch developments on screen. We are not minded to follow suit just yet.

The Cervantes Prize · On 23 April 2020 (the anniversary of Cervantes's death) Queen Sofia of Spain will present the 2019 Miguel de Cervantes Prize, the principal literary award in the Spanish language, to the Catalan poet Joan Margarit. The €125,000 purse is ample recognition of a lifetime's work.

Margarit is eighty-one years old. In his day job he is an architect, but he has published twenty four books of poetry, in Catalan first, but in Spanish also. This is not his first prize: in fact he has won many of the major Spanish-language awards available. Sharon Olds wrote in the introduction to his Bloodaxe collection *Love Is a Place* (2016) that his work is 'brilliant . . . sensually beautiful (but not too beautiful) and with a genuine, just-conceived feeling'. He is Spain's most widely acclaimed contemporary poet, at home and abroad. Bloodaxe published two earlier volumes, *Tugs in the Fog: Selected Poems* (2006) and *Strangely Happy* (2011).

Whitman in Bolton · A celebration for Walt Whitman's 200th birthday was held in Bolton in May, including readings, a Whitman walk, specialist talks and a display of Whitmaniana at the Bolton Museum (part of the touring British Museum exhibition, Desire, Love Identity: exploring LGBTQ histories in Bolton, 15 March to 26 May). All events focused on commemorating the great poet's connection with Bolton, begun by a group of 'Whitmanites' in the 1880s. The major event was a two-day conference held at the University of Bolton, 23-24 May. It featured keynote addresses from Kirsten Harris, Michael Schmidt and Don Share. The conference culminated in a reading of Whitman's poetry at Bolton Central Library. Readers included Share, as well as poets James Arthur, Tim Liardet, Kathryn Maris, John McAuliffe, Jennifer Militello, Maurice Riordan, and Ben Wilkinson, alongside performances from local groups 'the Wonder Women' and women from the 'City of Sanctuary' group.

From the Archive

Issue 151, May–June 2003

SHEENAGH PUGH

From a contribution of six poems including 'Learning Hindi', 'Pride' and 'The Curator and the Art of Concealment'. Fellow contributors to this issue include David Kinloch, Edwin Morgan, Alison Brackenbury, Marilyn Hacker and Robert Minhinnick.

THE STREET OF SMALL HOUSES

Wooden booths, just big enough for one,
leaned close on a street stifled

with caraway, saffron, aniseed.
The old men pattered out on their errands

for food and firewood in the peppery air,
sneezing. They were foreigners, clerks

to the spice merchants, settled
among strangers who slowly turned

into neighbours. They went shopping
for small amounts. The city forbade them

marriage: they might live
and trade, but leave no mark.

On the Street of Small Houses
windows were paned

with horn or skin: scant outlook
for the old bachelors.

They got handy about the house,
used to long silences,

fond of their own company. They grew
apart from each other, lost their language

for one in which they would never
take vows or christen children.

Of Pine Trees and Silence

VAHNI CAPILDEO

When we took the six pine trees home from the Ministry of Agriculture show in Port of Spain, they were hardly a handspan high. The tiny trees had been planted in Styrofoam cups, as if they were no more expected to survive than the unfortunate goldfish sold in transparent plastic bags of water at school bazaars. Transplanted in a row along the north boundary wall of our yard, they shot up. Their bark became tough and rusty. Their branches registered each puff of the north-east trade winds.

The hush and whoosh of the pine trees' tossing joined the overtones in the symphony of sounds that meant 'neighbourhood'. Lonely dogs were louder, blended Irish/Trinidadian sneezing and laughter beneath a flapping laundry line was clearer, but the breezes filtering through silvery-green needles added their own presence, faint and insistent like foghorns from the port (in those years free of cruise ships), or the dusk and dawn chug-chug of lions from the zoo at the foot of the hill.

Silence, a sound engineer in Sheffield once explained to me, really means the absence of unexpected sounds. In his work on historical programmes, he often had to remove the deep mechanical reverberations of our post-industrial ways of living, thus (re-)creating the impression of a stiller time, in which birdsong shrilled, and the revelry within a hall or active worship in a church would roll out, attractive and shocking to a lone and humble walker. Isn't 'silence' also the presence of expected sounds?

The stories with which we grow up are part of the internal soundscape which we experience as normal or regular life. So the trees (five, since one died off) found themselves written into our games, and especially our reading. We half-expected to find Piglet shyly chatting to Winnie the Pooh, or, later, Sinis the pine-bender stringing up his victims between two trunks and being caught out by Theseus. Later yet, or perhaps all along, what with the sometimes bluish undulation of the Northern Range as a backdrop, the pines fused in our imagination with the landscape of Bollywood film – that is, with the appropriated landscape of Kashmir.

The impossibly long legs of a youngish, black-clad Amitabh Bachchan striding through pinewoods in the falling snow was one of my earliest images of A Poet. In Yash Chopra's iconic *Kabhi Kabhie* (1976), Bachchan's character wins the heart of a beautiful girl by reciting poetry. They spend a lot of screen time making out chastely to a gorgeous soundtrack with genuinely well-crafted lyrics, in the unnamed, Edenic setting of Kashmir as fetishised by the Indian film industry. On the night of her arranged marriage, as her doting bridegroom ceremoniously removes her jewellery piece by piece according to time-honoured Hindu romantic tradition, the poet's ex weeps prettily, and mentally plays back a yearning version of his verse. As ever, Kashmir itself, 'the world's most densely militarized region' (www.standwithkashmir.org), remains convenient for the projection of Indian (and Pakistani) fantasy, an area of silence.

August 5 was never going to be a good day for me. My paternal grandfather died that day in 1990, of a heart attack in reaction to a coup in the Trinidad whose independence he had fought for once upon a time. I remember his full-body struggles to breathe, which resembled the actions of a man fighting the King of Terrors in hand to hand combat, at least as strongly as I remember anything else of those brief days of violence. August 5, in 2019, also became the day in which I renounced Hinduism.

It is, of course, impossible to renounce a system which is not a faith, but a way of life into which one is ineluctably born, a saffron dip underlying any subsequent desertion or baptism. However, I have come to realise that the unconscious display of ordinary signs of the heritage into which I enter at upper-caste level, let alone its intentional practice, can traumatize large swathes of the South Asian population, who have suffered at the hands of my kind. I have seen cringing, wincing, and flashes of fear in able-bodied, well-educated men, at the mere sight of a literary group in 'my' traditional clothing – entirely justified, because of what we are known to be capable of.

The everyday symbolism of millions, in the motherland and in the diaspora, has been nazified – cf. the carving of Hindu religious symbols into the bodies of sexually tortured women during the Gujarat pogrom in 2002, when Narendra Modi, now Prime Minister of India, was the Chief Minister of Gujarat. This nazification has valency, whether or not western spiritual seekers in Aum, lotus, and elephant god t-shirts, or western scholars talking about 'inscription' and 'writing the body', choose to make themselves aware of these hardly hidden facts.

August 5 this year saw India send tens of thousands more troops into Kashmir and impose a communications blackout, including landlines, mobiles, and the Internet. What is happening there? Well, tourists have been expelled, then visitors tentatively re-invited to enjoy, enjoy, enjoy; land protection laws have been overturned and development of tracts of forest is on the cards; foreign observers selectively have and have not been allowed in; an Indian fashion label launched a Kashmiri-style collection, while Kashmiris could not leave their houses, let alone ply their skills, or buy and sell; oh, and Genocide Watch has issued a genocide alert.

How would anyone know what is happening there? Use your imagination? One thing for sure: rather than organizing the independence referendum which the famously distinctive and historied Kashmir has sought for over seventy years, India has (with dubious legality or constitutionality) abrogated Article 370 of the Indian Constitution, which guaranteed Jammu and Kashmir's special status and a measure of self-determination. Why is international media not ablaze with this? Who knows? It is easier to silence 'paradise', with the vast hydroelectric potential of the Indus running through it, scary Muslims from Pakistan and (my also-ancestral) Afghanistan crisscrossing borders, and between two nuclear states.

The pre-Partition North Indian oral memory, or the knowledge running in my blood, which seldom makes it directly into my writing, found voice in my mother's words when she heard the news and the not-news about Kashmir. 'We are the same people,' she said with bewilderment and hurt, about the atrocities. 'Kashmir has always been its own place,' she then said, about the occupation. To feel that kinship in difference, without contradiction, would be to make modernity continuous with the only tradition that now seems worth claiming: one in which the sounds of neighbourliness are vital and alive.

Further resources, including books, films, a 'Kashmir syllabus' for education, resources for protestors, and talking points for faith groups may be found online, for example from standwithkashmir.org I have no direct connexion to any such organization, but, inspired by the richness of the works they list, I have returned to, or read for the first time, the work of Kashmiri authors such as Mirza Waheed and Ather Zia,[1] literature being the limited sphere in which, as a poet who is not tall, male, or a megastar, and who walks among very different pine trees, I weep and sing.

Centring Kashmiri voices is a crucial way of breaking, and hearing, the silence. If I cast this piece as memoir, it is from lack of political expertise; but the writings of experts, and Kashmiris, are readily available. To close, here are some lines from Agha Shahid Ali's 'Vacating an Apartment':

> They learn everything
> from the walls' eloquent tongues.
>
> Now, quick as genocide,
> they powder my ghost for a cinnamon jar.
>
> They burn my posters
> (India and Heaven in flames),
>
> whitewash my voicestains,
>
> make everything new,
> clean as Death.[2]

---

1 At the time of writing, work by Ather Zia remains online at www.scroll.in/article/807015/they-want-us-to-write-in-blood-four-poems-on-kashmir.
2 www.poetryfoundation.org/poems/43278/vacating-an-apartment.

Remembering Jim Atlas

JONATHAN GALASSI

In so many ways Jim and I lived our lives in parallel. We met in college, studied in England at the same time, married the same summer and moved to New York to pursue similar dreams, and raised our families in tandem. Typically, Jim made a story out of it – it was one of his many gifts: to shape experience into narrative. The Atlas version was that he and Anna invariably followed Susan and me in everything we did. It wasn't true, of course: Jim was always trailblazing while the rest of us lagged prosaically behind – but it was his incorrigible gift to see our lives historically, even as we were living them, and to give their scraggly, no-count odds and ends the patina of myth.

We were two outsiders – aren't we all? – who, when we were still boys, really, pledged allegiance to an old-fashioned faith in literature. I think both of us believed in writing as *the* way of making sense of things, knowing, living even, and we had the temerity and foolhardiness to pursue our commitment. Being males, we eyed each other a bit warily, each assaying his own travails and progress in relation to the other. That's what brothers-in-arms, comrades, boon companions do. 'Galassi!' he'd chirp, with a certain triumphant relish not devoid of irony, when I showed up – he was the only one of my friends to call me by my surname. It must be a Midwestern habit, I told myself. Whatever the reason, he had me pinned, and we could get down to the serious games of dishing, enthusing, worrying and wondering that were the currency of our life together.

My first memory of Jim is seeing him cross Harvard Yard in a long green raincoat and galoshes, carrying a stuffed pea hen and a large sepia photograph of Castel Sant'Angelo. Even as a freshman, he made a big impression. He was brash and enthusiastic, with a nasal Chicago accent, a big, toothy smile, and a disconcerting lack of deference for Eastern manners and mores. Nothing cowed him – not even the manic, Olympian Robert Lowell, who held court at his notorious Office Hours where he commented, often witheringly, on the poems submitted for criticism. I didn't dare go near the place, but Jim barged right in and soon established a rapport with the great man. I didn't know then that Jim had an unusual arrow in his quiver: his doctor father actually yearned for his son to be a literary intellectual – an exceedingly rare reverse-Oedipal gift. Jim didn't throw his father over and become an investment banker, though. By our sophomore year he was president of the *Advocate*, the student literary magazine that went back to T.S. Eliot and Conrad Aitken, handing it on to me when the year was up with a nonchalant behind-the-back pass. Been there, done that.

The point is that Jim had endless reserves of panache, fearlessness, and energy. He had scads of girlfriends and was a crack tennis player to boot – no wonder he was a shoo-in as a Rhodes Scholar. It was in England, in fact, that we became real friends. I would take the three-hour bus ride from Cambridge where I was studying, hungry for a taste of the lively Oxford life Jim seemed to be leading. Or we'd meet in London, for sonnet-writing contests and other po-biz, as he called it, diversions.

Judith Thurman, another great friend from those years, reminded me recently of our visit to Jim early in 1972, soon after his hero John Berryman's chastening suicide. Jim was studying, prophetically, with Joyce's biographer Richard Ellmann and living at Boar's Hill, the storied haunt of Matthew Arnold, Robert Bridges and John Masefield, cooking up projects for the fledgling Carcanet Press run by his friend Michael Schmidt, who went on to be one of the poet-publishers of our generation.

But Jim was too much of a live wire for Oxford, it turned out. He moved back early to the real Cambridge, where he made the most fateful and brilliant score of his life, winning the love of Anna Fels, who would be his inspiration and source of strength for close to fifty years. By the time I turned up again, Jim and Anna were ensconced in a house in Concord with Richard Sieburth and Anna Cancogni, more or less re-enacting Lowell's great memoir poem, 'To Delmore Schwartz' – the one that starts, 'We couldn't even keep the furnace lit!' Before long, Jim had embarked on a biography of Delmore – 'I never heard anybody call him Schwartz,' as Dwight Macdonald said. This is the single thing I admired most about my friend: that he undertook a truly game-changing project on a wing and a prayer, with no visible means of support but an innate faith in his ability to carry it off. And he did it. He wrote a great book, with the guidance of Dwight and the testimony of a whole generation of New York intellectuals who were only too glad to come upon a young person who saw magic in their hardscrabble, idea-haunted lives – and who would prolong their relevance for another decade or two. No one in our cohort has done better. His biography of Delmore – I always thought it should have been a musical, too – was definitive; it recalibrated American literary history and was a National Book Award nominee. Not bad for someone still under thirty. It thrust Jim into the midst of New York cultural life, the A-list as he loved to call it. Try getting there with a poet's biography today.

Then came the culture wars. Jim was deeply embedded. He did it the old-fashioned way: working at *The New York Times*, *The New York Times Book Review*, *The New Yorker*, at Tina Brown's *Talk*. He was virtually the last of the old-fashioned literary penmen, publishing a novel and reams of criticism, profiles, occasional essays, and eventually another major biography, of Saul Bellow, whose *Humboldt's Gift* in some respects echoed Jim's Delmore. The vicissitudes of their cat-and-mouse relationship are hilariously and movingly recounted in Jim's marvelous last book, *The Shadow in the Garden*, in which he deconstructs the biographer's dirty secret: that the real subject of a biography is always the one who's writing it.

But he was always restlessly inventive. Later on he had the effrontery to become a distinguished publisher, devising and editing several successful series of brief lives. For a while he even – horrors! – went to work with Amazon – something we agreed not to discuss. No, we didn't always see eye to eye. Jim could enjoy mixing it up with friends and foes. It was Anna, and Molly and Will who were the great constants in his occasionally topsy-turvy world; he and Anna were always real home bodies, living since the mid-seventies on the same block of West 77th Street and retreating to their place in North Bennington, Vermont, which became a beloved touchstone for their friends as well.

What was constant between us was the bond of our shared beliefs and affiliations – which became our history, as he'd foreseen. We'd put our chips down long ago on the same table, and they'd stayed there. Each of us knew what the other was up to, and why. The shorthand of our exchanges remained constant. The afternoons we spent together this year were among our best – full of gentle headshaking about the waywardness of life and work, which invariably resolved into laughter – sardonic and rueful at times, but always infused with the joy of being together.

Jim's failing and fading were incredible, incomprehensible, tragic to watch. It made me feel – maybe others do, too – that I'd taken him for granted. He was part of the wallpaper; of course, he'd be here as long as were. And he is. I told Will soon after his father's death that Jim is still with us and always will be. That is undeniable. We can all feel him in the room stirring things up with the nervous, electric, mischievous joie de vivre he never lost. I'm told he was working, helping friends, writing, planning, up to the very end. But it's also true that his passing has left a gaping hole, not only in his family but in all our lives. Jim is here but also, astoundingly, he has left us, and the unfairness of his untimely departure is impossible to absorb. One can only hope that with time these terms will reverse, and the comfort of his enduring presence will somehow mean that his absence hurts less.

He was one of a kind and deeply loved, and he won't be forgotten.

Here is the last poem I wrote for Jim this past spring (I'm afraid I stole some of its details for these remarks):

BOOKWORMS

It wasn't just the wide brown misted view
of Castel Sant'Angelo in its Eastlake frame
and the stuffed peahen
you were humping across the Yard;
it was the raincoat and galoshes, too,
and your air of pulling a heist off,
intelligence poised like a harpoon.
But everything was sepia then
that wasn't Technicolor.
You, ringleader of the Bookworms,
gunning for the kingpins in their fifties
who couldn't keep a fire lit
but their suns enflamed the horizon.

Boar's Hill, sonnet contests in dim pubs,
Dwight's dacha with his pinned-up undie ads,
wives in the pool, wives in the mirror, kids –
we dove into the molehill, chasing our tails,
bowling for a strike that might raise us
into word heaven.
You wrote books that were instant sepia.
No one clocked the dads the way you did,
irksome white guys nursing their injuries
like tantalizing
tumblers of Dewar's.

I don't know what happened to the pea hen
but the castle hangs in your dining room
where I've wolfed down a lifetime
of game birds in sepia sauce
and gazed at the battlements
of Eighty-first Street. Your shelves
are crammed with books, no room for another.
Who rehearses the old grievances,
who covets the brown furniture we lived by?
Where is word heaven, Jim?

Letter from Wales

Sam Adams

Rhys Davies – a writer's life (Parthian, 2013) was one of the late major achievements of Meic Stephens's own exceedingly busy career as writer and editor. It won him the 2014 Wales Book of the Year non-fiction prize. Meic brought to the task his vast accumulated knowledge of Welsh writing in English, familiarity with M. Wynn Thomas's pioneering article on his subject with respect to covert homosexuality in a symposium on Davies's work, *Decoding the Hare* (2001), which he edited, access to letters and other archival material, and long friendship with Lewis Davies, who was able and willing to confide a wealth of personal reminiscence about his brother Rhys. Lewis, the last of his family, already deep into his seventies, living comfortably in a flat in Lewes, Sussex, and contemplating mortality, was determined his money would not fall into the hands of HMRC, for him embodied in Mrs Thatcher, whom he execrated. I have previously given an account (*PNR* 209) of how he and Meic thwarted the PM by setting up a charitable trust in Rhys's name to do worthwhile things for writers and writing in Wales.

As a biography of this elusive figure who ranks among the foremost twentieth century short story writers in English, Meic's book is unlikely to be superseded. That much understood, one may still be intrigued by an occasional by-way. I was struck by the information, gleaned from Lewis, that some of the money donated to the Trust (finally amounting to substantially more than half a million pounds) came from Alice B. Toklas via fellow American Louise H. Taylor. There aren't many unfamiliar with the name Alice B. (for Babette) Toklas, and her partner, as we would say, Gertrude Stein, whose memory and literary reputation she preserved devotedly through the years between Stein's death in 1946 and her own in 1967. Few will not have seen and wondered at the photograph of Gertrude in the large studio of the apartment at *27 rue de Fleurus*, Paris, which she shared with Toklas from the early 1900s, the walls densely hung with rows of paintings, many instantly identifiable, like Picasso's 'Fillette à la Corbeille Fleurie', sold a few months back in the Rockefeller sale for $115,000,000. In her will, Gertrude named Alice her heir, but the collection of paintings was to be for 'her use for life' and thereafter pass to her nephew Allan and his children.

Judging from photographs, Alice was not the most prepossessing of life-companions. In a 1915 passport renewal application she described herself as follows: Age: 37; Stature: 5 feet 2.5 inches; Forehead: Low; Eyes: Hazel; Nose: Aquiline; Hair: Black; Complexion: Dark; Face: Oval. Descriptions of her appearance by others invariably mention her moustache and are often unkind. Those who knew her well were impressed by her quiet charm, her warmth and affectionate nature, and her astute judgement in the arts from painting to dress design and cooking. *Staying on Alone* (1973), a selection of her letters from the period after Gertrude's death, edited by Edward Burns, also reveals a colourful and gossipy correspondent.

The passport application tells us Alice was born in San Francisco on 30 April 1877. She was the daughter of Jewish parents who initially said they had emigrated from Germany, though at the 1920 Census her father, Ferdinand, declared he was a retired dry goods merchant who was Polish and spoke Polish. Presumably, post-World War I, with Poland once more independent, he was proud to reassert his nationality. He had begun his business career in Seattle, then moved to San Francisco and made the family prosperous. In 1890 they moved back to Seattle and Alice continued her education at the Mount Rainier Seminary. There she fell in with girls of similar tastes and interests, among them Louise Hayden. Although Louise was five years her junior, Alice would certainly have known her, because, outside school, as talented pianists they shared the same teacher, Mae Potvin, who had a high reputation in Seattle and put on concerts at which both performed. In December 1892, for example, when Miss Potvin's pupils performed at 'Pettis' Chambre de Musique', Alice Toklas, who was fifteen, played Schubert's Impromptu in A flat and the precocious ten-year-old Louise Hayden the first two movements of a Beethoven Sonata. For a time they kept up their musical studies, Alice having lessons from concert pianist Otto Bendix and graduating in music at Washington University, and Louise acting as assistant to the far better known Isidor Philipp in Paris, before both abandoned all ambition in that direction.

Hayden came from an army family. Her father was Major James Rudolph Hayden, who is described as 'one of the pioneers of Washington'. He was manager of the 'People's Savings Bank' and had a 'handsome' home on Boylstone Street. When he died unexpectedly of pneumonia, in November 1902, the *Portland Morning Oregonian* reported Louise and her brother, Lieutenant John L. Hayden, had returned to Seattle for the funeral. In Paris, in 1918, she married Emmett Addis, of Hartford, Connecticut, who had become a Lieutenant Colonel of Infantry during World War I and later served as Instructor at the Army General Staff College. Marriage took Louise back to the US, but during her time in Paris she had attended the salon at *27 rue de Fleurus*, met Gertrude Stein and renewed her childhood acquaintance with Alice Toklas. They became firm friends, as the affectionate warmth of Alice's letters reveals. Louise visited Paris most years and gifts were exchanged.

Addis, recently retired from the army due to ill-health, died in Boston in 1932. In 1939 Louise re-married, in Taunton, Somerset, again to an army officer, Captain Richard Harold Redvers Taylor, known as 'Red', who was eighteen years younger than his wife. His army career had culminated in 1937 in a posting as Assistant Military Attaché at Addis Ababa, but with the outbreak of war he was recalled to serve in the War Office. There he met Rhys Davies, also doing his bit for king and country. Red had artistic tastes and as it transpired artistic ambitions. After the war he became a painter and sculptor of recognised quality, with exhibitions in London galleries and at Kettle's Yard in Cambridge. Like Gertrude and Alice in Paris, Louise and Red welcomed writers and artists to their London flat in King's Court North. Rhys Davies who never aspired to much more than a humble bedsit, was a regular at this salon and sufficiently trusted to be allowed to use the flat when its owners were away to entertain young guardsmen.

Lewis Davies suggested the relationship between Louise and his brother was particularly close. When she died in 1977 she left half her estate, some £65,000, to Rhys, the other half going to short story writer Bill Naughton. Did this include money left her by Alice Toklas? Louise was executor of Alice's will (some sources say her adopted daughter), but all agree in her declining years she had little personal wealth. Even the precious pictures were taken from her. While seeking relief from crippling arthritis at a spa in Italy, and living there in a convent (she had converted to Catholicism, which, she was assured, allowed a heaven where she would be reunited with Gertrude), the widow of Allan Stein had the entire collection seized and locked away securely at the Chase Manhattan Bank in Paris. But Louise did receive a waistcoat and two brooches that had been worn by Stein. One of the brooches is of lapis lazuli; the other, of coral in a silver setting, which appears in the iconic portrait of Stein by Picasso, was of monumental significance for Alice, harking back to her first meeting with the love of her life. Louise donated the brooches to the Fitzwilliam Museum in Cambridge; the waistcoat she gave to Rhys, who sold it for £100 early in 1978 to the University of Texas. When Rhys died intestate in August 1978, the net value of his estate, £80,000, came to Lewis, the one survivor of his family, and he, by care, frugality and shrewd investment, built up the capital and with extraordinary generosity gave all away to the memory of his brother.

Footnotes in Songs and Poems

WILLIAM POULOS

The average scholarly edition of a Shakespeare play looks something like this:

Romeo[1]: But soft![2] What[3] light[4] through yonder[5] window breaks?[2][6]

Below a passage (or even a line) you'll find footnotes explaining obscure words, historical context and literary allusions. Unhappy being confined to the bottom of the page, the empire of footnotes now usually colonises at least half of it, and it's not that rare to find a page with more notes than text. Sometimes these notes are helpful; sometimes they're crucial to understanding the passage. Sometimes they're bewildering, and after reading them I discover I know *less* about a passage than I did before.

That song lyrics don't come with notes is a mixed blessing. Most of the time, though, they don't need them. The lyrics of, say, Gershwin, Porter, even Morrissey at his most pseudo-literary, don't need explaining because they are drawn from common experience rather than the annals of literature. An obscure word or an allusion can be a nice ornament because it isn't the driving force of the song. Songwriters, in fact, know that their audience isn't going to look anything up, so they ensure the context clarifies any obscurities. Now that we have many scientists contributing to public discussions, one would expect more scientific vocabulary to appear in songs and poems, but despite some notable exceptions, such as Stephen Edgar, few poets have yet been able to integrate a scientific vocabulary into a poem that's widely read and recited. Where William Empson failed, Tim Minchin succeeded. Minchin's brilliant song 'You Grew on Me' is perhaps unbeatable:

> You grew on me like a tumour
> And you spread through me like malignant melanoma
> And now you're in my heart
> I should've cut you out back at the start
> Now I'm afraid there's no cure for me,
> No dose of emotional chemotherapy
> Can halt my pathetic decline
> I should've had you removed back when you were benign...
> You grew on me like carcinoma
> Crept up on me like untreated glaucoma
> Now I find it hard to see
> This untreated dose of you has blinded me
> I should've consulted my local physician
> I'm stuck now forever with this tunnel vision
> My periphery is screwed
> Wherever I look now, all I see is you.

The ideas of love as a disease and of a speaker not being able to see anything but his lover predate Jesus Christ, but the modern scientific vocabulary revitalises them. The lyrics work so well because you don't have to look anything up, and if you didn't know that a glaucoma affected your eyesight before, you do now. Unfortunately, modern songwriters use fewer words than their predecessors and are more content with cliché and banality. One genre of music, however, has given us a lyrical vitality to match its musical vitality: heavy metal.

Sure, there are probably thousands of metal songs about death, dying, and killing, but in which other genre of music will you find:

> Come, blessed Dionysus, various nam'd,
> Bull-fac'd, begot from Thunder, Bacchus fam'd.
> Bassarian God, of universal might,
> Whom swords, and blood, and sacred rage delight...

You might know this as the Orphic hymn to Dionysus Bassareus Triennalis, but it's also part of the lyrics for the song 'Daimonos' by the Polish death metal band Behemoth, whose songwriter 'Nergal' spent six years studying history at university and is a qualified museum curator. (Behemoth also adapted the chorus from Swinburne's *Atalanta in Calydon* for their song 'Before the Aeons Came' – a rather unexpected reception for the purple poet, although the metal band shares his interest in taboos.) To the uninitiated, Behemoth sound like a malfunctioning jet engine, but metalheads appreciate their combination of Middle Eastern tonalities with the traditional fast tempos and highly distorted guitars. The problem with their lyrics is that they're far too detailed for songs: the anti-Christian sentiment is expressed through references to the occult and to figures from ancient religions. It's too much for the non-specialist.

Still, the intellectual stimulation that metal bands provide shouldn't be underestimated. I was an exceptionally torpid schoolboy who read nothing except guitar magazines, but I learned a lot of English vocabulary by listening to European metal bands. I was (and still am) a great admirer of the Swedish band Opeth; I listened to their song 'Serenity Painted Death' constantly:

> White faced, haggard grin
> This serenity painted death
> With a halo of bitter disease
> Black paragon in lingering breath

Haggard, serenity, paragon – was this English? I had heard nothing like this from the American and English metal bands I was listening to. I memorised these new words and started using them everywhere, much to the consternation of my teachers. In interviews, many of the European metal bands said that they had learned English by reading books, which probably explains why their vocabulary was much wider than the bands made up of native English speakers. For years now Salman Rushdie, both as a writer and as an editor, has emphasized how writers from the sub-continent have galvanized English fiction. If the comparison isn't too grand, I would suggest that European bands have done the same thing for heavy metal lyrics.

On a Shoestring

Poetry in the Blood: Celebrating 20 Years of Shoestring Press

BARRY WOOD

Small presses – like little magazines – have been essential to the health and diversity of poetry for the past century or more. They present a complementary and often counter culture to the products of mainstream publishing houses and are dedicated to the promotion of new and undiscovered talent and the revival of the work of forgotten and neglected older writers. They often depend on the energy and commitment of individual editors and reflect the editor's taste and character. Looking along my bookshelves I realise how much they have contributed to my pleasure and education in poetry over almost sixty years. They rise and sometimes fall and occasionally challenge the hegemony of larger, London-based publishers; but mostly they nurture their awkward independence and keep on keeping on.

Shoestring – founded by John Lucas in 1994 – is one such press and *Poetry in the Blood* marks its first twenty years in successful operation. The book brings together a group of twenty writers – mostly with some association with the press – with an invitation to write an essay about a poet whose work has, in a phrase by Robert Hass, 'gotten into their blood' and to illustrate in a poem how the chosen poet has influenced their own creative and critical practice and approach. The results are varied and stimulating and give an unusual insight into the relationship between reading and making. To give some examples: Clare Brant and Christine O'Neill acknowledge a profound debt to Rilke, and Brant gives a particularly poignant account of how recovering a 'soggy and burnt' copy of Rilke's poetry in the debris of a house-fire helped her through the disaster. Lawrence Sail and Gregory

Woods pay tribute to the poetic wealth and 'dryness' of Auden; Helen Nelson is not entirely convincing on the 'simplicity' of Ruth Pitter, but Merryn Williams makes a good case for re-opening the book on Charles Causley. Angela Leighton provides a fine essay on Les Murray which became part of her highly original study *Hearing Things: The Work of Sound in Literature* (2018); and Tony Roberts on Lowell and John Lucas on Edward Thomas show how another poet's influence can be deep, surprising and specific.

But what of the other products of the press? From its Nottingham base the press has always pursued a robust regional outlook without being merely provincial. It has wider perspectives. Central to the commitments of the press has been, on the one hand, the publication of mid- and late-twentieth century poets whose work is out-of-print or unjustly neglected and, on the other, contemporary British and American poets and work in translation. Among the first group is the work of Anna Adams, George Fraser, Iain Fletcher, Maurice Rutherford and Vernon Scannell. The publication of Nicholas Moore's *Selected Poems* (2014) is a particular triumph. The volume opens with his 1940s and '50s poems ('Ideas of Disorder at Torquay', for example) and incorporates the famously eccentric thirty versions of Baudelaire's poem 'Spleen: *Je suis comme le roi d'un pays pluvieux*'. Printed as a sequence, Moore's versions of 'Spleen' show an extraordinary versatility and inventiveness and make much better sense in the context of Moore's work as a whole; and the body of Moore's original poems demonstrates among other things the creative impact on his work of his early reading of Wallace Stevens and W.H. Auden.

A group of contemporary writers is more various in content and style perhaps although there are continuities through an interest in jazz, for example, and the influence from modern American poetry. This group includes the work of Jim Burns, Malcolm Carson, Richard Kell, John Gohorry, Angela Leighton, Janet Montefiore, Christine O'Neill, Michael Waters, the Romanian poet Michaela Moscaliuc, mainly translated by herself, the Russian poet Eugene Dubnov, translated Anne Stevenson, and the Israeli poet Miriam Neiger-Fleischmann, translated Anthony Rudolf.

The work of Janet Montefiore, John Gohorry and Tony Roberts gives a fair representation of the scope and diversity of the press. Probably better known for her critical writings such as *Feminism and Poetry* (1987), Montefiore's sequence of fifty sonnets *Shaping Spirits 1948–1966* is sharply observed, original and unsettling. Despite the title the poems owe more to Wordsworth than Coleridge in their use of childhood memories and sometimes specifically in the imagery; ice-skating with her sister on the Cam she pictures 'a fish motionless as a fly in amber / beneath us as we slid past willow trees / black against sunset staining ... / snowy fields and rigid broken reeds'. And there is perhaps a bow to Adrienne Rich in these 'snapshots' of an awkward and frustrated scholarship-girl: 'I lurked in an unwanted solitude / furiously pulling up an empty sieve / from a dark stream where nothing good could live'.

John Gohorry's *Thirty-Three Ostrich Cadenzas* is a sequence of twelve-line poems in unrhymed tercets with an epigraph from Beckett: 'Any fool can turn a blind eye but who knows what the ostrich sees in the sand?' The sequence is a surreal fable based on the meltdown of the nuclear reactor in Fukushima on 11 March 2011 in which seven ostriches were set free from a local zoo. Gohorry creates a post-apocalyptic struggle between 'the autonomous Ostrich Republic' and the world of officialdom more interested in cover-up than clear-up. It is imagination against bureaucracy, aepyornic ingenuity and solidarity against spreadsheets and indifference. Gohorry retains the quirky humour of Marianne Moore's sardonic 'He "Digesteth Harde Yron"'– to which he alludes – but the humour is darker and the ending tragi-comic, cruel and absurd.

Tony Roberts published his first book *Flowers of Hudson Bay* with Peterloo Press in 1991. When the press folded in 2009 he was taken up by Shoestring who published his second collection *Outsiders* in 2010. Since then he has flourished partly because of his retirement from teaching and partly because of support and encouragement from his new publisher. His excellent *Drawndark* came out in 2014 and this was followed by two collections of essays – many of which first appeared in *PNR* – which with a breadth of insight and refreshingly jargon-free style show a substantial knowledge of nineteenth and twentieth century British and American poets. As a poet his models are Browning and Lowell, suitably adapted to his own character, identity and themes; and as a critic he acknowledges a debt to the unfashionable Arnold. (See the splendid 'Matthew Arnold in New York, 1883' in *Drawndark*.) His most recent collection is *The Noir American & Other Poems* (2018). The title poem is a narrative sequence which attempts to describe the world of African-American jazz musicians in New York and Paris in the 1950s. It's an ambitious project and may be mainly interesting and comprehensible to jazz aficionados. It suffers from some rather over-expository passages and awkwardness in its impersonation of the spoken idioms of the time and milieu. But the poems build into a graphic, complex and convincing portrait of the turbulent lives of jazz musicians of the time: inner emigres at home and exiles abroad, facing hostility and prejudice – even in the more relaxed atmosphere of Paris – at great cost to themselves and their art. The elegiac tributes to Parker and Billie Holiday are unsparingly accurate and moving. The poems in the second half of the book exemplify the range of Roberts's technical skill, humour and plain honesty; for example: 'Worms', a gently ironic poem of marital love; 'The Isle of the Dead', a beautifully spare lyric on mortality; and 'In An English Country Garden', a comic ode on the intrusion of a family of rats into suburban life.

Shoestring is now in its twenty-fifth year and in the past year has published a pamphlet of *14 Poems* by the poet and translator Anne Beresford, John Harvey's stylishly produced *Aslant* with photographs by M.E. Boiling, new collections by Martin Stannard and Malcolm Carson and a bibliography of the work of the poet, 1890s Yeats scholar Iain Fletcher. Against the odds, the press thrives.

Sheila Wingfield

from Finnesburie to Enniskerry

JOHN CLEGG

Here is Sheila Wingfield's 'When Moore Field was all Grazed' in its entirety (first published in her 1964 collection *The Leaves Darken*):

When Moore Field was all grazed
And Finnesburie ploughed,
People were firey, clever, glum, or crazed; [ed: 'fiery?']
Hard knuckled; and proud
Liars; and well-phrased.

It's appealed to me since the first time I read it; Wingfield had from the beginning of her career a gift for Yeatsian diction (sometimes verging on Yeatsian pastiche), and this was Yeatsian in the best sense, earning that final 'well-phrased' for the author as well as the 'people'. But it's also subtler than I initially gave it credit for.

The poem was probably written in Ireland; Wingfield was the Viscountess Powerscourt, and her home until 1963 was the enormous Powerscourt estate. Ireland and the Irish landscapes are preoccupations throughout her work, and I'd initially taken the two place-names in the poem as local to Powerscourt (or at least personal to Wingfield) – although that un-Gaelic termination '-burie' should have been a warning. In fact, of course, they are familiar London place-names, Moorfield and Finsbury. Wingfield may well have encountered the spelling 'Finnesburie' in Holinshed's *Chronicles*, while she was researching her genealogical poem 'Origins'. (Holinshed: 'At the comming back of the lord protector from his iournie into Scotland [...] the maior and aldermen [...] met him in Finnesburie field'.)

The poem is not, then, a piece of straightforward nostalgia or plaint against urbanisation, as (say) James Stephens might have written, and as I first read it; the valorized time it describes is not Wingfield's childhood but the sixteenth century, and the list of temperaments in the third line resolves into the humours of sixteenth-century astrology. It metamorphoses into a terse epigram on a historical period. But I think it has a further subtlety up its sleeve.

Moorfield and Finsbury were both heavily targeted in the Blitz; I think we are meant to hear the 'razed' in 'grazed', and fully register the connotations of 'crazed' and 'firey'. At the back of our minds, we should have a paraphrase like, *In the war, after central London had been flattened back to ploughland, the popular attitude took on some characteristics of the sixteenth century mindset* (which was obviously used to dealing with catastrophe). If I'm right, and this is an oblique war poem, it is not based on any direct experience – Wingfield spent the war comfortably ensconced in a Bermudan hotel. But it allows 'hard-knuckled', 'proud / Liars' and 'well-phrased' to ring as generational plaudits, which is surely true to our first reading of the poem: she's clearly praising *something*.

'Adam', from the same collection, is shorter by two words, and also has its own unexpected depths:

Poor Adam! Marrying
A screech-owl before Eve was made
And liable to meet God walking
Slowly, in the humid, dusky glade.

Here, though, I think the additional context is biographical. The poem was first printed in the *TLS* of 26 September 1962; I suggest that the poem's Eden is Powerscourt, and its occasion was the realisation that, in order for a divorce, the estate would have to be sold. (As it was - to the Slazenger family, of tennis racket fame – although they eventually ended up marrying back into the Wingfield family.) The first two lines are a self-deprecating sneer; 'screech-owl' is the Viscount's attack against his wife. 'Dusky' – used now and again in *Paradise Lost*, in the same way, to signal what's encroaching – gives the atmosphere of impending expulsion. (*Milton's God* by William Empson had been published the year before, and I think its descriptions of the scenes of Adam and God conversing in the garden may have also been at the back of Wingfield's mind.) But the other adjective in the final line, 'humid', I think is pure Powerscourt – Enniskerry in County Wicklow, which Powerscourt sits just to the west of, is one of the dampest places in Ireland. In an earlier poem, Wingfield had described 'a country house / Where a clammy mist falls over the garden, / Fills muddied lakes / And surges into the guest-room.'

I find these short late poems much more compelling than Wingfield's early forays into imagism, or her long poem *Beat Heart, Beat Drum*, praised by Herbert Read and G.S. Fraser. Still, Fraser, in his introduction to her selected poems (*Her Storms*, 1977), was quite right to reach for Landor as a comparison to Wingfield at her best. She is happiest, like Landor, with the epigram or riddle or lapidary phrase; she was hard to get on with; and her work is underrated through being piecemeal, very varied in quality, and hard to classify.

From the Journals

3 May 1998

R.F. LANGLEY

Another reading in Cambridge last week, with all the circumstances in place... the drive there after school on Friday after a quick bowl of soup... traffic jams to start in, so I go to the Wall roundabout to avoid having to cross the lane as I would have had to do had I cut across by Mill Cottages... and was glad I'd done so since the lane was full of almost-stationary cars... solid jams and fast jostling at the brief episode on the motorway, then the long unencumbered run across, nowadays without towns or villages, and the difficult parking around Sturton Street so I end up with the car a street away from the house.

The practice reading to Nigel and Ewan Smith in the evening, after we had listened to Perelman in the Keynes Room... I found that, sitting back under the balcony, I couldn't hear him and followed nothing, though those alongside were chuckling... so, as I thought, I am quite deaf now. The copies of *Jack** were there on the table in the Chetwynd Room, Rod Mengham seeming anxious that I should be pleased, relieved that I was... cream cover with the three black outline grass moths, exactly as I'd drawn them and run them off on the school photocopier, clean and clear so their forelegs, which don't touch, don't blot together at all.

Things as a whole seem as neat and tidy as they should be, but the anxiety about the reading, the worry of not hearing, the hurry of quick stops and accelerations on the drive, the slur of many miles swept past, the infinite detail of the Wheales' house, objects on every surface, pictures cramming walls, the intense darkness of the front room where I sleep, its curtain as thick as a carpet

JACK

R.F. LANGLEY

and the street immediately outside so it needs to be kept drawn or you are face to face with a passer-by, their demon doll pegged up in the sitting room, naive works next to sophisticated, cats on couches, the dog fidgetty, watching, woofing, all my past Christmas cards framed and up by the sink, so many people I half know at King's... I am aware I am not registering.

I have an idea that three Jack poems will fill the half hour if I first say a word about Jack, then introduce each with three biographical/referential facts... drag in a touch of Marion Milner, Wittgenstein, the pigeon in Tournus, the vesper flight of swifts, John Anslow in the cloakroom at Shire Oak *(Grammar School)* forty years ago, asking me what we were doing there as he suddenly saw absurdity.

'R.F. Langley's reticence of output has not prevented

---

* *Jack*, a pamphlet of five poems published in 1998 by Rod Mengham's small press Equipage, later included in Carcanet's *Collected Poems* and *Complete Poems*.

him becoming respected among younger poets for his exemplary construction of near-abstract epiphanic realisations' the programme says. Who wrote that? Which younger poets? I've tried out a possible sequence twice... once with my evening Art History class – but I filled the whole evening then, explaining, then with the Lower Sixth S Level group... coming closer to the required timing. With Nigel and Ewan I get near it... just too long on the initial remarks, Nigel says.

So – Saturday morning, 11 a.m., Helen Macdonald first, with interruptions from late-comers. At Stoke I couldn't hear her three years since, because she whispered. Now she sits easily, leaning forward, looking up often, and smiling, relaxed, and opens up much more. Her poems are less dense too. Delicate and adroit. A fine affair.

And I'm second, before the interval, leaving Michelle Grangard, with Peter Riley translating, for afterwards. A low step up on to the stage. Chair by the grand piano. No extra notebooks... all I need are in my red folder, and, of course, I never look at anything but the poems, having the rest in my own words by heart. Grab a way in... since Peter introduces me with the 'abstract epiphanic realisation' remark (so it wasn't he who wrote it – he slightly deprecates it)... 'Here come three epiphanic realisations' I say, and then tell them simply about Marion Milner and her sending out a part of herself when listening to music, and that part being the inception of Jack. I chop out the whole piece on Wordsworth's *Night Piece*, the 'pensive traveller' being different from the narrator's voice, neither and either being the poet, the analysis by Hertz from *Wordsworth and the Tears of Adam* which I used with the Art class and sixth form. That had already gone last night.

Now I am brief and simple and suddenly I'm talking, it's easy, it's not too naive, they are listening intently, they have paid money for this. There are about fifty of them but I'm conscious of only a few – Kate leaning out from the third row looking pleased, Out to Lunch's girlfriend right at the front, because no-one could miss her – and also she seems interested, John Wilkinson's baldness over to the right and Peter there too... the big black bust of Keynes to the left. I find I am reading the poems, not just the words, getting the run of the sense in my mouth, making nice decisions about how to say that this time.

And no stumbling with the introduction... quite jokey... and no-one else does this kind of thing nowadays... it's old-fashioned but still the best way in to my material... the given facts, the pigeon, the Arcopal bowl, and Ophelia with her shards and flints for charitable prayers... the swifts... Wittgenstein's brief bit on how we recognise objects we have seen before without making a comparison with an image we have in our heads... watching for the birds to rise out of sight each evening in Wenhaston... then John Anslow, absurdity, grass moths, the lavatory at the Ten Bells and Jack sent off to look things up in the library. Thank you. I'm standing up. They're clapping – hard – as before. It's obviously sufficed. Peter says my introductions ought to be published somewhere.

The rest of the day... some films... Roy Fisher, Peter Gizzi, Gig Ryan... walking in the college gardens along the river with Tom Lowenstein and Ewan... and a lady who teaches photography with Kate and used to live in Florence with Bob Walker and Ewan, clearly a lot of the past there... which I touch only at the edge. People punting, maladroitly, loudly, stupidly. Julia Ball, who has an exhibition in Bury St Edmunds, telling me she has been on a walk at Wicken Fen and stumbled over a grass snake and what a coincidence that is after my reading about grass moths, Tom thinking that grass moths are plume moths, and talk of a cloud of orange tip butterflies. The frogs in Nigel's pond, heads through the weed, throats pumping, letting you scratch their backs, a pond full, a house full, a weekend full, John Welch there, sleeping somewhere else, strolling in the dusk back to a car speaking of collecting coins.

The drive back on Sunday, after a brief visit to Peter's shop... car intact but the driver's window jams a little open... inexplicable... the fault disappears by the end of the journey... a sense of disconnection, happenings being unpredictable and taking place some way off, affecting me with an impact, but, though the impact touches me, stresses me, angers me, the actual event is outside by some distance and coming at it, be it interesting converse with friendly people or an invisible cause jamming the car window I am winding up with my right hand as I shoot along the Huntingdon road... coming at it is not possible... it stultifies me.

Edited by Barbara Langley, 23 November 2019

Intimacy and other poems

SASHA DUGDALE

Forest Fire

'They led a group of women prisoners past. The women saw the men and stopped. They wouldn't move. The woman guard leading them shouted: 'Come on! Get walking!' But the women wouldn't move.' – adapted from *Second Hand Time* by Svetlana Aleksievich

Nearing dusk, a band of women passed
In padded jackets, rags wrapped round their feet
They saw the men, stopped, would walk no further

The men leaned axes, saws against their flanks
And watched as the guard prevailed upon the band
In vain, until at last she hissed in disdain

Animals, and spat and turned away. Like deer
Then they came. She to him, not pre-ordained
But more like atoms bond, drawn to pair

And each one fell towards another and it was done.
He placed his arms on her. Felt her bones
The matchwood girdle of her pelvis, her light form

Her face, the missing teeth, the lines of dirt
But shining, in the sudden grip of
Things beyond her, things she'd always known.

They had no time. He nuzzled her, pulled her in
And she put arms around his waist
And unwound the string he'd kept tied tight.

She ran her nose across his skin
He trembled, his hands were blistered thin.
Her haunches were as white as water

He was afraid to cause her pain
But seeing how she longed for him
He pushed his finger deep in her

Like meteorites
Falling through the dark – the ground gave way
He held her up. She was so very light.

He tasted sweat and something like leaf-matter
Fur, woodfire, her bloody snout
Her eyes level with his throat

Her flickering gaze. Saw he was lamed
Alive, but barely, like the first hours after hibernation
She opened her mouth, her tongue flamed

All projectionists know that a still
For all its perfection, cannot be held
It catches instantly, it will incinerate us all –

In fire the creatures briefly met
Swayed silently among the smouldering trees
Sleek as stones on river beds

Then fled. No longer of this world:
Motley pairs, scorched, but free
Seeking place where life might take hold

Odysseus Welcomed from the Sea by Nausicaa

(Eric Gill's bas-relief at the Midland Hotel, Morecambe)

a deforming ballad

My bestie appeared in a dream and said
your room is a slum, used sanitary towels
curling on the floor, your clothes are fetid
Pull your finger out, girl, it's fucking foul.

So I asked my father: dad can I take the car
I've bagged up some gear for charity, I'll wash the rest.
And he knew right there what it was for
he knew I wanted to look my sexy best.

Dad laughed and chucked me the keys:
Take my car, sweetie, ask your friends.
Head down the beach, poppet, have yourself
Some fun, go for a spa with your hens.

Dressed up no one would guess our age
but on the beach we did all stupid stuff
threw the ball around, played at chase
Took all our clothes off.

Sometimes we can get silly like that
I mean, without drinking, and on our own
Unafraid, somehow, did I say that?
Just girls, no pressure, just us, alone.

And then this man rises out of the sand
Naked as fuck but shielding his prick
Filthy with gull shit, smelling so bad
I literally tasted sick.

We're screaming, running from his reach
Because who knows what kind of fuck
Wanks off watching girls on the beach
I was terrified, I thought I'd run out of luck –

I want to run like my fearful band
Streaming hair, screaming, naked as night
Twisting and turning over the sand
Like swallows in tangled flight –

But something drags me back by force,
Curiosity, or pity for him, or even shame
Or the gods, who put their fingers up your arse
Leave their claw marks in your brain.

Or maybe just: he's a man, I know my place
Or maybe just I want to be chosen
Or maybe I'm a freak I'll be erased
My bare arm   I'm frozen.

First amongst femmes
Or slut without shame
I stretch out my bare arm
I see my hand far   far   away

Like it belongs to someone older
A little clutch of prehistoric fingers
And something fluttered on my shoulder

Feathery-grey,
full of hunger

Did I say I was never a victim?
Although I was riven like a sea-rotted hull
Although he took my life and flicked it
Like a stone to the end of the world

I helped him with good grace
And inside I knew every complication
I learned to lie and it was bare-faced
On my lies they built a civilisation

Rewind:
tell my father
to close the gates and hurry
fly like birds
from the wreck on the sand

But most of all:
don't listen to his story
close your ears   draw back your hand

Intimacy

Just as when you unearthed a nest and all the tiny bodies
curled together touched the air and began their disintegration

clutching like children or lovers, and still furred or feathered
but only for that moment, already extinguished, near extinction

beginning to break apart, just as morning haze disperses
when the sun tips the hill top, so much dust held in simulation

and now disbanded, I know nothing means nothing,
that substances transform, still some shapes touch more than others:

nestling things exhibiting proximity in death. To have a mouth
and press it against another's wing, to spread a wing and cover

over a sac of flesh, that fools me, makes me soft and hurt,
the ache shaped from love for what is not, and worse,

for what will be no longer, so mourning is double-vapour
rising from false intimacy between one corpse and another,

already gone, all of it, a loosening image of life and love
an attitude struck by the dead, their dry palms

cupping air. Even so let fools rehearse it while they have
breath. The shiver when a touch catches us unaware

you carrying me to bed curled in your arms,
the still-warm mess of sheets, limbs, hair.

Dark Matter

The contents of the museum were moved to a bunker
and then disappeared. Old photos show us what was lost
a few black-and-white Old Masters taken at a distance

a grainy picture of a statue, hunched, ready for flight
the parure of a lost queen on a throat of ancient velvet.
Even the urge to speculate on their fate is muted now:

shipped out wrapped in sack, burnt or heaped over
with the gravel and rock of a dying city. The odd leads
trail into darkness, which is where the other nine tenths

of human endeavour end. The known world expands
but the world we buried grows faster still. Its statuary fills
a universe of mirrored halls, its songs echo soundlessly,

and tangled in the stars a thousand poets whose faces
lie smashed under battlefields. As we seek to perfect
the chord, the line, the divine form, remember

wax tablets, scrolls, scribbles on palace walls
trampled into strata, remember how porcelain
melted, remember there's an undone precedent

for everything we've done. Somewhere dark energy
is shooting coins from forgotten civilisations
into a jukebox larger than the sun.

The Resistance

NYLA MATUK

'AND SO THIS BEING THE TIME of manifestos, here is mine: that poetry, at its best, does not speak on behalf of the self. It speaks on behalf of the Other. It speaks on behalf of community. It speaks the self only in so far as the self is part of something larger,' Kei Miller wrote in *The Poetry Review* in 2017.[1] His declaration bears a resemblance to a number of ideas I grappled with as I prepared and edited *Resisting Canada: An Anthology of Poetry*, published in September 2019 by Véhicule Press of Montreal. The twenty-eight contributors address a plethora of ills resulting from the statecraft of a settler-colonial enterprise, i.e., Canada. Miller's manifesto takes up poetry's capacity to bear witness – perhaps to injustice, or to a measure of social agency. It underscores a distinction between the enduring legacy of the egotistical sublime of the English Romantics – 'on behalf of self' poems and confessional poetry, which narrate an individual, and poetry with a view to collective consciousness, a politics not necessarily exclusively of identity and identity's fraught subjective realities, but telling 'history from below,' of a collective identity ready to present such a history.

Many of the poets I included in the anthology address the myriad ways Indigenous Peoples, who lived on the land called Turtle Island before colonisers arrived from Europe, have been dispossessed. They still live here, and they are still being colonised. The poets examine, *inter alia*, the fallout of shameful Canadian institutions such as residential schools, and the violence against Indigenous women and girls that is a legacy of the originally racist assumptions that accrued over decades and centuries. The imperialist mindset led to stealing and settling lands, acts of violence and betrayal perpetrated by white people from Europe. The long history of stealing from, and/or destruction of, First Nations, Métis and Inuit peoples' lands, customs, mythologies, and languages, was informed by Europeans' doctrine of *terra nullius* – a belief in the existence of a land without people – and the ethos of Biblical manifest destiny, wherein Europeans gave themselves divinely-ordained rights to colonise.

I started work on the anthology while I was conducting the research for a long biographical essay that examined the roots of my parents', and my own, relationships to the Canadian state. I began to make sense of why my father, a Palestinian from Jerusalem born during the colonial British Mandate period (1918–48) might find himself living in Canada. The question also arose in connection with my mother, who was born in New Delhi, India, before the end of the British Raj and lived through the sectarian violence of the partition of the subcontinent. Her lineage is half Afghan (Pashto) and half Turkish. I didn't need to read too far into these histories to discover the very long shadow cast, from the transfer of populations, onto a colonial place like Canada. My parents' story begins with ethnic cleansing operations in Palestine and India that resulted from geopolitical strategies for separating people into states that were conceived of along the lines of ethnic and religious identity and demographic manipulation. This dangerous project continues in Palestine today and less visibly, against minorities in India and in other countries around the world. Kashmir, under military occupation as of September 2019, is another territory in the grip of colonial strategies whose machinations were concocted at the time of the partition of India. Creating displaced, stateless and refugee populations or forcing immigration to North America, the geopolitical maneuvers – which went hand in hand with the dispossession of people from their land, the de-development of their cultural and civic identities, cities, infrastructures, and natural environments – have yet to be reckoned with in full.

The poems I selected are not about cultural or ethnic *personal* identity; they consider social conditions created by the settler-colonial state and how such conditions may impinge on identity, or attempt to erase identity. As I started to think about the effects of resistance poems, I also began to question the frequently drawn distinction between, on the one hand, poems of private consideration (such as those communing with nature, an object of romantic love, or other *loci* of meaning English language readers often associate with the English Romantics or the American Transcendentalists), and poems of public concern in which political agency and resistance are the subjects, akin to Kei Miller's 'something larger'. The anthology represents the return to concerns with collective identity at a time when concerns of personal identity seem to dominate as a mode for poetry published today, particularly in the United States.

But the 'something larger' Kei Miller developed could also engage a writer's political agency. It need not circumscribe resistance, but may be about insisting on existing, on not going away. In a 2018 conversation with author Dionne Brand in the *Literary Review of Canada*, the Michi Saagiig Nishnaabeg political theorist, poet, and activist Leanne Betasamosake Simpson – a contributor to the anthology – underscored the creative power of bringing personal and political agency to writing while disregarding the need to be understood and the expectation of accommodating those who have colonised and estranged one's people: a refusal of erasure:

'Wider audience' is code for white audience, which is code for less angry, less political, more palatable. It means paying

---

1 Kei Miller, 'And this Being the Time for Manifestos.' *The Poetry Review* 2017: 107 (1). 33–35.

attention to the experience of a white person reading my work with very little knowledge of the Indigenous. It means privileging the experience of a white person reading my work over Indigenous readers. Making sure that I'm making my point without offence. Paying attention to tone. Having a glossary so 'everyone' can understand the Nishnaabeg words. Removing insider knowledge and layered meanings. Being concerned with such things produces different work. It limits the stories you can tell and the way you tell them. It limits the worlds you can build. I've always been drawn to writers that reject this premise. I like reading books where Indigenous lives and worlds are affirmed. Where we are not victims or feeding victim narratives. Where we open up worlds, not close them down.[2]

In one of her contributions, 'Remembering Mahmoud, 1976,' the Stó:Lo Nation poet Lee Maracle invokes the Palestinian national poet Mahmoud Darwish[3], as well as the affinities between the struggles of Indigenous Sioux and Oglala Lakota and Palestinians, all of whom have been murdered by settler-colonial state military (the United States and Israel, respectively). Both Maracle's tears and her daughter's presence signal a personal engagement to a larger collective, referencing the 2008 and 2014 attacks on Gaza, and the 1890 and 1973 massacres at Wounded Knee, South Dakota:

-40 Celsius in Winnipeg
Palestinians and Indigenous children wave placards
Stop killing children in Palestine
Free Gaza
My tears freeze on my face
my daughter is there
just as she was there 35 years ago
Chanting Free Palestindians
my frozen tears cut pain lines on my face
...
I whisper Palestine, Palestine – Free Palestine
Wounded Knee, no more Wounded Knees

A similar personal/political distinction collapses in Darwish's work, where his resistance to Israel's disenfranchisement of his people is often lyrically delivered via the articulation of a personal inwardness. In his study of Darwish's quest for poetic agency, *The Poet's Art and His Nation*, the poet and scholar Khaled Mattawa observed, 'The evolution of Darwish's poetry constitutes a struggle to preserve the poet's presence within political deliberations and to maintain and develop the aesthetic pursuit that grants the poet the degree of independence upon which his relevance as a discourse-maker depends.'[4] Liana Badr has observed that 'the relation of Mahmoud Darwish to poetry is best defined in the metaphorical way he defined it himself by comparing it to 'being at home.' He says, 'The metaphorical home which the poet creates for himself is an internal home invented by the poet himself. It is a kind of a poetic verse. So, home becomes a poetic verse.'[5]

Following a tradition of Palestinian poets who were incarcerated for their engagement in what is called the 'Arab Revolt' against the colonial British Mandate in the 1930s, Darwish was imprisoned specifically for poetry-related activity no fewer than five times; his crimes included travel to do a reading without Israeli permission, and the publication of a poem in a newspaper. From the Israeli Defense Forces razing his village in 1948, when he was a child, to the illegal Israeli settlements around his burial site today (he died in 2008), Darwish's resistance to the Israeli state spans both his life and death. In 'Identity Card' he repeats the lines, 'Write it down! / I am an Arab' in mockery of the Israeli administrators who demanded, for racist purposes, his identity, and their use of the non-specific term 'Arab' rather than 'Palestinian,' purposefully, to underscore the attempted erasure of Palestine, a repeatedly colonised country. What Darwish experienced, however, is far from over. Recently, poet Dareen Tatour, an Israeli citizen who is Palestinian, was tried and imprisoned/house arrested for close to four years for a poem she posted on Facebook. As of September 2019, she has been cleared of all charges.

This tells us poetry can still be a potent threat to the denialist cultures of settler states. While my examples are from the US and Israel, the dehumanization of the Indigenous other is alive and well in the settler-states of Canada, the US, and Australia. Coming up against the Manifest Destiny and biblically inspired ideas of pioneering and settling land, artworks invigorated by the experiences and perspectives of the oppressed go some way in raising the consciousness of non-Indigenous people to unsettling facts: children abused and killed in Canada's residential school system; the current high rates of suicide in Indigenous communities; the incarceration of Indigenous Peoples and allies for resisting corporations and governments; over 1,500 murdered or missing Indigenous women and girls; the lack of clean water on reserves; the Trudeau government's recently launched judicial review of a human rights tribunal order requiring the government to pay the families of Indigenous children who died as a result of underfunded foster care. The tribunal found the government to have 'willfully and recklessly' endangered Indigenous childrens' lives.

'Indigenous Peoples,' the Leanne Betasamosake Simpson has said, 'whose lands are occupied by the Canadian state are currently engaged in the longest running resistance movement in Canadian history; one that predates the formation of Canada itself.'[6] Any opposition to violence perpetrated by the state – on humans or the environment – should take cues from these various Indigenous resistances. Their steadfast persistence

2 Dionne Brand and Leanne Betasamosake Simpson in conversation: 'Temporary Spaces of Joy and Freedom' *Literary Review of Canada*, June 2018.
3 Darwish was first published in English by Carcanet.
4 Khaled Mattawa, *The Poet's Art and His Nation* (Syracuse, NY: Syracuse UP, 2014), p.12.

5 Liana Badr, 'The Impact of Place on Identity in the Words of Mahmoud Darwish' in Mitri Raheb, ed. *Palestinian Identity in Relation to Time and Space* (Nazareth: Diyar, 2014), p.86.
6 Leanne Simpson, 'Oshkimaadiziig, the New People' in Leanne Simpson, ed. *Lighting the Eighth Fire: the Liberation, Resurgence, and Protection of Indigenous Nations* (Winnipeg: ARP, 2008), p.13.

against an attempted genocide, and their words and actions of radical empathy for the land, may be tracked in a plethora of forms: blockades, strikes, gatherings, occupations, and installations. Writing and reciting poetry are other important ways of disrupting or signaling acts of environmental destruction, ethnic cleansing, and hollow Parliamentary apologies and recommendations. To discuss in particular the *disruption* and *resistance* of poems, I believe, is to remain steadfast against the demand from colonizers to respect a colonizer agenda, e.g., to capitulate to what is known as 'recognition politics'. In Canada, an official government policy of 'multiculturalism' is one form of recognition politics, which pays lip service to respecting ethnic difference while doing nothing to alleviate the ongoing destruction of Indigenous Peoples.

The political scientist Glen Coulthard, a member of the Yellowknives Dené First Nation, draws on the work of the revolutionary thinker Frantz Fanon to show how recognition conferred to the colonised 'without struggle or conflict' is not real freedom, but rather a kind of foreclosure of the realization of freedom. In this scenario, 'the structure of domination is modified, but the subject position of the colonized remains unchanged – they become "emancipated slaves".'[7]

In her study of Kahnawà:ke resistance, Professor of Anthropology Audra Simpson, a Kahnawà:ke Kanien'keha:ka, asserts that the alternative to the paternalistic politics of recognition/multiculturalism is *refusal*. Turning the Canadian philosopher Charles Taylor's 'ethical good' of multiculturalism and diversity on its head, Simpson writes that 'refusal comes with the requirement of having one's political sovereignty acknowledged and upheld' rather than be relegated to the status of a claimant of rights and land.[8] Poet and storyteller Gregory Scofield, with roots in the Métis of Kinosota, Manitoba (a community established in 1828 by the Hudson's Bay Company), makes use of the idea of self-determination – *katipâmsôchik* – 'The People Who Own Themselves', when he writes, at the close of 'Policy of the Dispossessed,' 'In that part of the country / we were always *katipâmsôchik* – / and our displaced history / is as solid as every railroad tie.' The poet and writer Beth Cuthand takes owning oneself into her politics of refusal as well, in her poem 'Post-Oka Kinda Woman'. With a rightful sense of entitlement, she ironizes settler place-branding, which was built on capitalism:

> She's done with victimization, reparation,
> degradation, assimilation,
> devolution, coddled collusion,
> the 'plight of the Native Peoples.'

> Post-Oka woman, she's o.k.
> She shashay into your suburbia.
> MacKenzie Way, Riel Crescent belong to her

like software, microwave ovens,
plastic Christmas trees and lawn chairs.

The collective, public, political struggle doesn't prevent a politics of resistance driven by one's subjective experience as a witness, agent, victim, or dreamer. One of the best recently released books of poetic resistance is Claudia Rankine's *Citizen: An American Lyric* (2014), a sequel to her *Don't Let Me Be Lonely: An American Lyric*, published a decade earlier. Using the second person, Rankine's witnessing of anti-Black racism in quotidian urban situations allows readers an empathic glimpse into how an individual is beset at every turn, in ordinary life, with systemic oppression. In the United States, this oppression is present as the legacy of both slavery and settler-colonisation; it is the same racism I see in Canada's history of colonial activity. Like Rankine, Billy-Ray Belcourt, a writer and scholar from the Driftpile Cree Nation, has used second-person observation to depict a system that refuses to stop its destructive and industrial development. The encounter Belcourt describes in his poem 'The Oxford Journal' distils hundreds of years of resistance to a single, disturbing exchange, rendered in an elegiac-toned prose. It's also significant that the exchange takes place in England, the most powerful of the colonising entities that came to Turtle Island. The sudden switch to first-person narration toward the end of this section of the poem underscores the uncanny nature of this moment, a brush with erasure and the poet speaking the truth of 'history from below':

> You are called 'wonderfully exotic'. A man looks at you, tilts his head,
> and presses that you are 'too mixed' for him to pinpoint any sort of
> ethnic belonging. This is a world-threatening feeling: to be so other
> that you barely exist in a place whose imperial conquests sought the
> destruction of your people. When you tell him you are native he
> doesn't say anything. He lets the silence do the talking, as if he were
> lamenting the violence that went into producing
> someone like you. I can tell he has heard a thing or two about us.

---

7 Lou Turner quoted in Glen Coulthard, *Red Skin, White Masks: Rejecting the Colonial Politics of Recognition* (Minnesota: U. of Minnesota P.), p. ix.
8 Audra Simpson, *Mohawk Interruptus: Political Life Across the Borders of Settler States* (Durham: Duke UP, 2014).

Two Poems

BRIGIT PEGEEN KELLY

Music

On this side of the dunes, there is no wind. On the other
side, the sea side, the wind comes across the water, and
always, soft or hard, it blows. But on this side, even when a
little wind finds its way here, you can hide from it,
because in back of the dunes, which are like pyramids, great
white pyramids, there are many small dunes, the dunes'
offspring, and in the small dunes there are countless
windless hollows in which you can lie down and listen to
crow cry and the low sound of the sea. There is a gun
range, too, on this side, tangles in barbed wire, but no
guns are ever fired on it, and so on some days the grey deer
leap over the wire and graze on the grass, though the grass
is sparse and yellow, and sometimes they sleep in the
old stands of stunted trees. I like to think of this, the
sleeping deer lying down next to the sleeping guns, like the
lamb and the lion, as if those caged acres were part of a
better world. On this side of the dunes, the sand is
soft, and it is so quiet, the wind blocked by the sand, and
the sound of the sea dampered, so that it sounds like muffled
organ music, or retreating thunder, or sometimes I think it
sounds like swarming bees, and then it seems there must be a
giant hive hanging over the sea, a slowly swinging hive
swollen with insects and honey, and maybe sometimes the
honey falls down into the black water below, and that is a
good thing, because the black waters are bitter, and maybe
in some lights sailors can see the honey in the swells, and
be comforted, as we are comforted by the unending hum. But
it is different on the other side of the dunes. The sound
is different. If you climb the largest dune – and it is a
hard climb – for the dune is high and steep, and the sand
pulls at your heels, when your head at last rises above the
sand, the wind hits your face, soft and hard, and the sound
of the sea, a sound that was a moment ago sweet, is so loud,
magnified beyond reckoning, it almost drives you to your
knees. And it is as if you have been deaf all your life and
then someone rips the stoppers from your ears and you hear
not the thing you imagined music to be – something like the
wings of a bird as it dives and circles which seem to be
both part of the bird, and something that has captured the
bird's shining body and is carrying it away – but all the
world's music, all of it, the drums, and trigons, and harps,
and sackbuts, and whistles, and cymbals, and chants, and
dirges, and rattles, and love cries, and paeans – crashing
before you. And it is unbearable. It is unbearable. But
still, you want to run toward it, or run into it, and maybe
be tossed in the air like a bird, or have your head drummed
against the sea's sandy floor, but more than that you want
to run back to where you came from. And why not? Didn't
some poet say that, or some condemned man? Better the
windless hollow, where you catch your breath, and curl
on your side like a deer, and maybe, after a time, according
to your own lights, fashion from what is at hand a little
Jew's harp, and begin to play.

Outolintu*

for Pirkko Markula

Lepers are outolintu, of course, but there
are not so many lepers now. And none
have bells. The bells of the lepers have gone.
And someone who steals your parking place
is outolintu, or someone who steals
the one you love. But in that case you
are outolintu, too. Sitting with your parrot
on the stoop... A spittoon on an altar
is outolintu. As is a gun in a nursery.
A dictator is outolintu for the people
he rules, and the people are outolintu
for the dictator. Not even people, but something
else altogether, penguins, say, or worms.
The poor are always outolintu to some.
As are the maimed, or those halt of speech.
Ham at a bris is outolintu, though there
is a Yiddish word that covers that circumstance
better... Sometimes when you see yourself
in the past, you realize you are outolintu now,
but were not then. And sometimes you
long to *be* outolintu, out of it all,
away from the fuss. A brass door on an igloo
is outolinto. And an arrow in a gun
is a mistake. As are the wheels of a bike
on a car. A Freudian slip is always outolintu:
the guest who shows up uninvited. And
laughter at a funeral is sometimes outolintu,
as is the one who laughs, and sometimes
not. It depends on the circumstances.
Some actions are outolintu. Selling rabbit's
foot key chains at an Assembly of Atheists,
or cutting off your own head. Some days
are outolintu; for example, the Day of the Dead,
a day of celebration for an uncountable
number of outolintus. Sometimes it pays
to be outolintu. The one who misses by minutes
a plane that will crash. Or, like Saint Francis,
the one who chooses to disrobe in church.
Sometimes it seems that we, like the dead,
might all be outolintu. A befuddled race.
One that was left in the wrong place.
Clearly, we can't take care of ourselves.
We seem to lack the proper equipment.
Perhaps we could repeat the word outolintu
as a kind of mantra to restore us
to sanity: outolintu, outolintu, outolintu,
let us learn to, let us learn to, let us
learn to be good.

* *Outolintu*: Finnish for strange bird; also refers to a person or thing that does not belong,
that is outside or 'other', or has been transplanted into a context that is not 'natural' to it.

Bright Wings and other poems

BEVERLEY BIE BRAHIC

Bright Wings

'Space, in all directions, can be distinguished into parts
whose common boundaries
We usually call surfaces;
And these surfaces can be distinguished into parts
whose common boundaries
We usually call lines;
And these lines can be distinguished into parts we call points.

I will lift up mine eyes unto the hills...

'Hence surfaces do not have depth, nor lines breadth,
nor points dimension,
Unless you say coterminous spaces penetrate each other
As far as the depth of the surface between them,
namely what I have said to be
The boundary of both or the common limit;
And the same applies to lines and points.

'Moreover, spaces are everywhere contiguous to spaces,
And extension is everywhere placed next to extension,
And so there are everywhere common boundaries of
contiguous parts; that is,
Everywhere surfaces act as boundaries to solids;
And everywhere lines in which parts of the surfaces touch;
And everywhere points in which the continuous parts of lines
are joined together.

'There are everywhere all kinds of figures,
Everywhere spheres, cubes, triangles, straight lines,
Everywhere circular, elliptical, parabolical,
and those of all shapes and sizes,
Even though they are not disclosed to sight.

'Space extends infinitely in all directions.
For we cannot imagine any limit anywhere
without at the same time
Imagining that there is space beyond it.
And hence all straight lines, paraboloids, hyperboloids,
And all cones and cylinders and other figures
Continue to infinity and are bounded nowhere.'

Newton in *De Gravitatione* writes and I recite
to myself like a Psalm:
I will lift up mine eyes unto the hills
This August night as I sit looking across the creek,
its bed in this season dry,
The sequoias and pines that bound it,
The hills, and the ocean that I don't see
but know is beyond,

At the innumerate stars, some of which turn out to be planes
Beginning or ending their journeys
On one of time's great circle routes.

Viktor's Pack

Girth of a punching bag
Gripped between his knees
Under the lunch table.
Beef and carrots dispatched
He will cradle it to
His shoulder like something
Ailing, and pivot towards
The door, pausing to run
His hands his large useless
Hands, under the cold tap.
Opens the small-paned door
And December howls in.
La porte! the others cry
In French, Romanian,
Polish, Polish. But the
Spoons speak only hunger.

The Library

Arriving in London from Manchester,
Walking towards Kings Cross Station
And the rail line to Hackney,
I skirt the walls of the British Library
I've been meaning to visit;
But my wheelie bag is recalcitrant.
We'll just peek at the piazza, I vow,
Then at least we can say we've been.

So, yes – I go in – see children
Scrambling over Isaac Newton
Holding his compass, heedless
Of ants; cuneiform like tracks
Left by birds in dried mud,
Read Magna Carta and then
I stop for lunch under a cliff
Of books, feeling as if I sit
In a seam of sand at the base
Of a canyon
Of human time, with my sandwich
And compostable goblet of wine.

Democratic Rags

On the 'democratic' in contemporary poetry

ALEX WYLIE

'These days power has to dress up in democratic rags in order to get what it wants and to keep what it already possesses.'
— Andy Croft, 'On the Poetry Industry: Stripped Naked by the Flames', *PN Review*, 45:5, May–June 2019

IF DEMOCRACY is indeed a lie, as Errico Malatesta claimed, then it is a lie we tell ourselves. Sold to ourselves as entrepreneurs, self-developers, influencers, advertising is our propaganda – precisely because we deny the possibility of a democratic propaganda as a kind of contradiction in terms. And if 'the truest poetry is the most feigning', as the clown Touchstone remarks in Shakespeare's *As You Like It*, what are we to make of a 'democratic' poetry in the light of Malatesta's claim? Through this Malatestan-Shakespearean lens, there appears a strange double bind at the heart of a self-avowedly democratic poetry: democracy is a lie that works on the basis that it is the truth, and poetry is a truth that works on the basis that it is a lie. From this (admittedly contrived) point of view, one might suppose there to be an ambivalence, or even a cognitive dissonance, at the heart of an aggressively propagandised 'democratic' poetics.

Writing this in the third year of the ever-deepening democratic crisis in the UK effected by the EU referendum – a crisis anything but democratic in practice – it seems like an opportune time to say something about how notions of democracy and the democratic have pervaded UK poetry over the last few years. I mean by this much of the poetry which is readily reviewed at the moment in print and online, which wins prizes, which is promoted in the mainstream media – and which has certain characteristics, crucially a disingenuous political 'authenticity' which flatters its audience (which manifests itself both in form and in sentiment), making it flavoursome to media ever more committed to content than discontent (if you'll pardon the pun). I will refer to it for these reasons as 'mainstream poetry': though this designation, as I will argue, runs counter to its promotions and self-conceptions. Claims, and assumptions, about the democratic nature of contemporary poetry abound; but the championing of such mainstream poetry in these terms is predicated upon an at-best-nebulous notion of what 'democratic' means, and this notion in contemporary poetry, literature, art, politics and society is built on a fantasy of the agency of the reader, or citizen.

Currently, there is a common objection to poetry of the past (and some of the present): that it is 'elitist'. The obvious rejoinder to this is that a representative democracy is intrinsically elitist, in that the constituency elects a professional politician to speak for it. 'Elite' can be defined as 'A person chosen for an office': an obsolete meaning, according to the *OED*, but one which speaks to the fundamental disavowal at the heart of mass-marketed conceptions of the 'democratic'. We are part of a political culture which is inherently elitist and yet which encourages the condemnation of elitism, or wilfully misrepresents it. The

citizen of the neoliberal democracy desires comfort and ease, but at the same time wants to *feel* like an agent of public and private power; essentially, it's not freedom that is wanted but the feeling of freedom. When Michael Gove remarked in the lead-up to the referendum in 2016 that '[p]eople in this country have had enough of experts' (Mance, *Financial Times*, 3/6/16), he was cynically manipulating this democratic fantasy. What Gove said translates as, 'Of course, you're the boss – so leave everything to us.' This is exactly what people want to hear; but such a statement only works if both speaker and listener act as if it is a statement of general empowerment, an operation possible through the effect of a pervasive cultural-political position of disavowal (*Verleugnung*).

The Oxford-educated, prize-winning poet Jay Bernard recently claimed (in the national media) that people's knowledge of poetry used to be predicated (probably) on their having received an 'elitist' education, and that this (probable) fact has begun to be challenged by a demand for a more 'democratic approach' to poetry in the last few years. (Freeman Powell, *BBC News* website, 28/1/19) It is a nice problem, however, to consider whether an Oxford education constitutes an 'elitist' one. I am not attacking Jay Bernard here, nor do I have a problem with people reading English at Oxford (aside from a Blackpool baby's jealousy, perhaps) but am simply trying to draw attention to what seems to me to be a confused and confusing – and I do think at times wilfully confusing – conception of the 'democratic' and the 'elitist' in the UK's poetry world and political culture at the present time. Let it be said, I am aware of the arguments about academic meritocracy with respect to admissions to the University of Oxford; but I am also acutely aware that there is no such thing as a 'pure' meritocracy separate from social, economic, and cultural entanglements.

And another aspect of such anti-elitist trumpetings is the notion of accessibility, a.k.a. 'Great art and culture for everyone'. Recently, the Director of Literature at Arts Council England published a piece in *The Guardian* on the current 'generation' of poets, christened by her as 'the new poets':

At the heart of the dispute [about poetry and 'the democratic'] was this notion of 'accessibility' – and the question of whether heightened accessibility necessarily involves a blunting of the fine edge that is poetry's USP. Whatever your view, there's no doubt that, historically, the number of people accessing poetry has been low. In audience terms, poetry has long been the literary world's poor relation, at once revered as high art, the place where language works at its outer limits, and viewed as difficult and (that word again) inaccessible, only touching the lives of the wider public when it was wheeled out to mark births, deaths and marriages. (Crown, *The Guardian*, 6/2/19)

For the Literature Director to say that '[w]hatever your view, there's no doubt that, historically, the number of people accessing poetry has been low' is puzzling and is at best a present-centric inaccuracy, at worst a falsehood. The rhetorical arm-folding '[w]hatever your view, there's no doubt that' smacks of someone winding up to tell a whopper to a credulous listener. Consider, for instance, the audiences of Elizabethan and Jacobean poetic drama, the droves that bought Byron's and Tennyson's books, Homer's and Sappho's fame in the ancient Greek world and beyond? Or, in more recent times, the sales, the cultural impact, of Wendy Cope, Philip Larkin, Linton Kwesi Johnson, Seamus Heaney, Elizabeth Jennings, T.S. Eliot? The Director's statement seems keen to present a picture of Arts Council England coming to the long-over-due rescue of a minor and mismanaged art-form: a salient instance of neo-Fukuyamaist historical exceptionalism. Poetry is not, historically, a minor art-form (the novel has only been around for a couple of centuries, actually), but it may have been culturally marginalised by the very political conditions which ACE represents. The Director's statement also, ironically, makes assumptions about what poetry *is*. The very powers-that-be who are making magnanimous noises about placing poetry front and centre are the ones who, in that very noise-making, imply its marginality – in the sense of 'people accessing poetry', whatever that means. Mass media and state bureaucracy have imposed terms by which they judge poetry to be wanting – a situation characteristic of a neoliberal culture of debt-imposition, performance metrics, and hedonistic guilt.

My objection is not to these individuals in particular; my objection is to a rhetoric of poetry-advertising which trades on facile conceptions of the democratic; indeed, to a mainstream poetry which is itself suffused with the pseudo-democratic false empowerments of advertising. Both these statements, from the poet and from the Director of Literature at ACE, employ a contemporary popular sentiment which operates by dint of the illusion that it is unpopular and unsentimental. They bespeak a cultural centrism which works through its self-promotion as progressive, even radical. And there is a broader political point that many of the people currently trumpeting 'the democratic' seem to me, at any rate, to be part of what I would consider, and would always have considered, to be the establishment.

Much contemporary mainstream poetry, then, trades on widely accepted, even hegemonic, notions of the democratic. The 'hegemonic democratic' is not a contradiction in terms but acquires its cultural and psychological power because it seems to be a contradiction in terms. In the premonitory political essay 'Order and Anarchy', C.H. Sisson observes that '[politicians of democracies] share, or appear to share, popular feeling, and act as they do because of, or apparently because of, those feelings. They do not stand above the people and direct it: they usually like it to be thought that any other man [*sic*]... would have done what they did, had he been in office and had he the wit to think of it.' However, though this advances part of the picture of UK poets at the turn of the 2020s, I would add the following definition to complete the picture, from the same essay, in which Sisson describes 'the politician who is partly deceived by his own propaganda'. I think this is more accurate of many of these mainstream poets, who are partly self-deceived because they identify with a culture which sees itself as beyond or perhaps above politics – as post-political – just as many poems (and books of poetry) now seem to be aspiring towards the post-poetic, or present a poetry which is as unlike poetry as possible. (Though I am not cavilling here at real creative innovation.)

Our current political culture sees itself as one which does not produce, and is in some practical and moral sense beyond, propaganda (e.g. the BBC's much-vaunted 'neutrality'). Perhaps it is this sense of historical exceptionalism which circumscribes the 'pure play' or fake-political nature of much mainstream poetry today, a poetry which is part of the meta-propaganda of post-political neutrality. And perhaps most crucially of all, advertising gains its hold through this illusion of value-neutrality. In this sense, advertising is the apotheosis and emblem of our political culture as it is of much of the most prominent contemporary poetry. Much poetry of the last few years, perhaps especially the absurdist kind (a very prevalent and garlanded current trend), is 'partly deceived by' itself by dint of being produced by this culture of meta-propaganda. The fact that contemporary propaganda is euphemised as 'fake news' is part of this cultural disavowal of political cynicism. It is a euphemism which is not acknowledged as such, one which has emerged from the very powers that produced the 'fake news' in the first place. This kind of bizarre disavowal is the very form of neoliberal culture.

As a crucial instance, then, the contemporary absurdist prose-poem (and much of it *is* in a prosaic sort of anti-form), as anti-poem or post-poem, trades on the reader's self-recognition through the poem of themselves as clever enough to be in on the joke of the poem at the expense of 'poetry' as sacred cow, as elitist and exclusive institution. This is a trend initiated largely by the earlier work of Luke Kennard, as far as I can tell, with such prize-winning and media-prominent exponents as Stephen Sexton, Jack Underwood and Jenna Clake (for example).[1]

The reader is made to feel clever by these poems' overt banality. It is not the linguistic qualities of the poem

---

1 Books are available by all these writers; or, for a quick look-up, poems are readily available online. In an online semi-interview piece, Jenna Clake stated the following: 'In *Madness, Rack and Honey*, Mary Ruefle writes: "If art were about intellect there would be no artists there would be only intellectuals."' (www.poetryschool.com/how-i-did-it/how-i-did-it-eric-gregory-award-jenna-clake-on-the-cow-whisperer) Accessed 10/10/19. Aside from this not really making sense to me, I don't believe (do I?) that Jenna Clake really shelves her brain whenever she sits down to write: I think, rather, she is making the appropriate cultural-political gestures to get ahead, both in her poetry and in her online commentaries, which may itself be from certain points of view a brainy thing to do. After all, we have had enough of experts, apparently.

which carry its deeper impact in this sense, but its entire arrangement which includes this cultural background. In this respect it is like conceptual art; it is poetry as pickled shark. Such writing creates the fantasy of activity when in actual fact it relies on the reader's passivity. Such poetry (or anti-poetry) makes a great show of not leading anywhere and of eschewing 'traditional' affect and meaning, working therefore on the principle of disavowal, as an ironic joke which the reader gets at poetry's expense. In this sense, it is the literary form of capitalist democracy and individual personal pseudo-politics: it exploits, and is exploited by, the fantasy that the individual is active in politics and morality when this fantasy is the mask of their much more profound desire to be essentially passive and inactive – and to be confirmed, consoled, and justified in their passivity by this fantasy of personal agency. It is like advertising.[2]

The democratic crisis of Brexit, in the aftermath, at the time of writing, of an illegal suspension of parliament

by the current Prime Minister, continues to prove that the citizen is at the mercy of so-called democratic 'process' – a noun ever used in this context for its (now-increasingly dubious in this context) collocation with the adjective 'legal'. The aftershocks of the 2016 EU referendum's 'direct democracy' have shaken the British constitution almost to the ground. It is surely by now painfully apparent that our democracy operates, when it does, through the citizen's fantasy of participation which masks a deeper, guiltier yearning for the consolations of passivity. The citizen is a subject pretending to be a citizen, a spectator masquerading as a player – a situation I see reflected in the poetry which this society is raising as its emblems. Mainstream poetry, then, is increasingly coming to reflect a self-deception at the heart of our democratic societies. What is more 'elitist' than a cabal of elected representatives – or than a succession of unelected prime ministers? And to end where I began, I will imagine Errico Malatesta addressing this deadlocked culture – 'inviting our young friends to use greater precision of language, in the conviction that once the phrases are dissected they themselves will see how vacuous they are.'

---

2 Crime fiction is part of this phenomenon, too, hence its immense current popularity in books and on television, with its stock character of the transgressive detective, the fantasy of transgression and individuality being the concealed obverse of the confirmation, the re-affirmation, of the political order. Here is the reader or viewer as democratic voter, their fantasy of agency masking the much deeper (you might say primal) satisfaction of an appeased passivity. At the time of writing, there is a poster throughout train stations in the UK advertising the latest Lynda la Plante thriller, *The Dirty Dozen*, which bears this tagline: 'You don't know who they are or when they will strike... But only YOU can stop them.' The novel is a 'Jane Tennison thriller' and as such is a third-person narrative: there is no 'YOU' as such, other than in this sense of fantastic identification.

From the Archive

Issue 151, May–June 2003

CARMEN BUGAN

From a contribution of four poems including 'Evening', 'January, Holywell Cemetry' and 'Return'. Fellow contributors to this issue include David Kinloch, Edwin Morgan, Alison Brackenbury, Marilyn Hacker and Robert Minhinnick.

THE DAY WE DECIDED WE WOULD LIE

I buried the blown bloom of white lilac
Into the heart of spring, straight
In the middle of that unacknowledged pact.

And it woke up inside the gust of wind
Repeating its incomprehensible grief
In the window of the first winter without you.

I now send it to you in your country:
Don't tell me what you do with white lilacs on your
  doorstep,
On your table, on your windowsill, in your hands...

The Feeling Sonnets

EUGENE OSTASHEVSKY

17.
This is my totter. This is my other totter.
They play at dress and redress.
They are princesses. They wear prints.   They wear prints out.
Out of what. Out of line. Out to what. Out to tatters.
They, hey. Hey do they speak.
They speak a speak. They speak a speak of mines and takes.
They speak a speak of ekes and keeps. They speak a speak of rates and tears.
They speak a speak I speak of not speaking. Hey.
My totter totters across the room. My other totter totters across the room.
My two totters totter across the room. They take a stance.
They take a stance by happenstance.
Totter, I am tot to you. I am that, other.
Totter, I am tot to you. I am that, other.
I am that other to my totters.

19.
The word 'daughter' is an element of basic vocabulary.
Like the word 'hair'. Like the word 'eye'. Like the word 'ear'.
First I saw the top of her head, then her head. She made a face.
Then all of her came out.
I threw away her chocolate.
'Chocolate' is not an element of basic vocabulary.
It was bad to her teeth. It was making holes in them.
She hit me and scratched my arm. I felt bad.
She said she was a witch. I asked if she knew any spells.
'Yes.' Proudly. 'A. B. C. D...'
Spelling also makes things come out so they exist.
I exist. You exist. She exists.
The word 'exist' is not an element of basic vocabulary. It came in from the outside.
But that's alright. Let us let it stay here.

20.
BERLIN IS GREEN. It is made up of old growth and new growth.
A fire took place here, a conflagration.
It's called conflagration because it started with flags.
A flag is a mark. If there's a mark, there's a market.
I come from the market, make dinner, and engage in struggle.
It is a struggle to get my daughters to sleep. They sleep on bunk beds.
The bunk beds are contemporary. They come from Ikea.
They were transported by trucks. My daughters are transported.
There is a herd of unicorns asleep on the rug below them. They come from developing countries.
Developing countries are also known as emerging markets.
In markets that are already developed, philosophers say that unicorns do not exist.
There's only one step from the remarkable to the marketable, and the unicorns have taken it, object the people of
    emerging markets. (But the philosophers do not hear them.)
A marketing campaign at the airport says this city is 'Done with Walls.'
A ring of barbed wire around the airport ensures safety.

21.

My daughters fall asleep on June fourth.
How does it make sense to say 'rest in peace' to the dead.
What do those words even mean, in or out of their order.
And who are you talking to, they have no ears.
My salt daughters fall asleep on June fourth.
They fall sleep in Berlin, also an evocative toponym.
The dead are perpetually unable to fall asleep.
How does it make sense to say the dead this or that.
How does it make sense to say they died for the future (now present as the present or absent) or that they didn't.
How does it make sense, a rondeau.
Behold, the tanks have turned into factory outlets. Behold, the bayonets have sprouted ears of corn.
The policeman's baton now conducts an orchestra. Everything turned out for the best.
The dead stand perpetually outside the gate of heavenly peace.

22.

She is drowned already, sir, with salt water.
She was a-sailing to Lesbos with a company of her peers.
They had fled from the wars and were preparing to play suppliants.
Her town traded hands several times, being bombed by some regional players and one – or arguably two – superpowers.
She is an evocative pronoun. A pronoun stands in place of a noun, that is to say no one.
Let sirens sound for those who sink when a mountain summit arises out of the sea.
They feel their way to cultural capital, for it is fitting for the living to feed on the dead.
Is she drowned again in the waters of my remembrance of her? No. After one death there is no other.
My personal pronoun is the shield of Ajax.
It is made of eight bull hides stretched taut oven a man-size, rectangular frame.
I kill sheep in the middle of the night. O sheep, I mistook you for my enemies.
Sir, this image shows me wading into the waters not far from the mouth of the Dardanelles.
The inscription next to my figure says Adidas. It is making a reference to my bathing shorts.
The water is cold, as befits a common grave.

Voice Lessons: A Notebook

JEFFREY GRAY

IN PUERTO RICO, 1997, I heard Herbert Blau scream. It was deliberate, not a reaction to pain. He was showing us – in a classroom – how to make a sound that would seem to tear your vocal cords to shreds but actually would cause no injury. The context was Antonin Artaud – Artaud's commitment, devotion, intensity. The scream, Blau said, should come straight up from where you find it down inside; you let it emerge without friction or duress, even though its texture and import were all friction and duress. I don't know if anyone else was in the building apart from our group of a dozen or so. It was a long scream and extremely loud. Blau was 71 at the time, small and slight of build. The scream didn't shake or wrench his body; his face did not turn red. But there was no separation between him and the scream; his eyes looked up like a nursing baby's, his mouth was wide open. The scream left no space for anything else to enter your mind, not even the thought, which came later, 'This is outrageous – can anyone hear?' Or, 'Isn't this illegal?'

*

The flutist James Kincaid advised, 'Tone should never be too direct, or too natural.' He
   also said, 'Darken the bright notes, bring them into place.' More profound, if less useful, he said,
   'Plastic and impeccable, music is the friction of space against time.'

*

In the 1950s and '60s most poets and critics thought that rhetoric and oratory were the opposite of authenticity. This is by and large still the view today. Dylan Thomas was an exception. There was Voznesenski, yes, and Neruda, but they came out of a different aesthetic, out of other languages; their growling, weeping, and singing were forbidden in English. Listen to Voznesenski at the top of his lungs reading 'I am Goya!' Then listen to Auden reading his translation of that poem – dry, affectless, etiolated. In English, 'honesty' meant this flatness. Thomas was able to violate that aesthetic because of the popular image of the drunken genius he shared with other Celtic actors and poets, because he had the vocal sweetness and authority, and because that repressed poetic was struggling to return. There was no place for irony in 'Dead men naked they shall be one / with the man in the wind and the west moon.' But it would be impossible to write this today; in fact, it was impossible then.

Fast forward: generational change, with spoken word: bombast is back, bigger than one could have imagined. But it too is saturated with irony.

Among experimental poets, 'voice' has long been in disrepute. They live in those bad old days when all poets distrusted the voice.

*

I went to see a flamenco show tonight, at Estudio Oscar Quero, outside of Granada. Quero is the young man who leads and rehearses the group, and he is the principal dancer – a brilliant dancer, one of the best in the world, they say. The singer's name was Alicia Morales. It was a voice straight out of Andalusia – different from the church-muscled American melisma, more feral and desperate, pressing beyond where you would think it could go, the voice climbing like a vine, creating new space for every branching figure. There was a 10-year-old boy who danced in one of the longer pieces, with nine females, as if he were not a person but the latest vessel – old metaphor but the right one – for a tradition.

*

Ida Lupino's voice of burned toast. Sammy Davis's, soaring with risk. Richard Burton's ringing like a bell through his forehead. Chet Baker's, small, intimate, in tune – then, later, out of tune, still intimate. Today, singing as if speaking, on the radio, Melody Gardot.

*

Our friend Gary Bates read poems in a voice like Ezra Pound's, who'd got that style from Yeats: bardic, weary (long before he was old), druidic, with arcane, Celtic pronunciation. That was what Gary and his wife thought of as authentic, like their velvet clothes, calligraphy, Tarot cards, and opium. But they wanted to go *all* the way back. They once signed a letter in each other's shit, with thumbprints.

*

Latamey Neyshart, now in her sixties, has dubbed all female vocalists in Indian films for the past four decades. Hers is the most recorded voice in history.

*

Late on a summer afternoon, I'm driving south toward California, and a 1940s tenor comes on the radio singing 'To Each His Own', music I would have hated when I was young. Before long, the voice, the late sun across the fields, and the thought of Bev, who died young more than twenty years ago, and whose house I had looked for in Corvallis earlier that day, become one thing. Voice, red-golden field, and Bev, killed by a tree that fell in a storm. It takes a long time for the sense of this to fade. As it does, I begin to think how much I've been admiring V.S. Naipaul's prose, and how I can never hope to be that tough and unsentimental. How could one see like that, write like that – even given the beauty of that – and still hear music?

*

I saw Son House when I was 24 in a Quaker meeting hall in Seattle. The audience was all white college students or faculty and some suburbans, though not the Frank Sinatra and Dina Shore cocktail-set suburbans. This audience would be called 'hipster' today. Find love wherever you can. Hit the note however you can, James Moody used to say. With whatever you've got (Donald Rumsfeld).

*

Adenoidal thinness of the voices of contemporary newscasters reflects the public's suspicion of the big male voices of Walter Cronkite and those who followed. Their suspicion, more than that, of knowers.

*

Gurjinder was turned down for the teaching job at Santa Monica College because he spoke too faintly. He went out and hired the most famous voice trainer in Hollywood. After a week, he was allowed another interview and a class demonstration. As he had been instructed, he vibrated the bones in his head and could be heard easily in the back row. He got the job and has worked there for thirty years.

*

Joan Baez was inducted into the Rock 'n' Roll Hall of Fame last year, amid the Vegas-Goth rockers clamoring for authenticity. In her youth you could say Baez's voice had the 'authority of sadness,' as Philip Larkin once said of Stevie Smith's poems. Now, she sings with the 'shreds of her voice' (Frank Bidart's 'Ellen West' on Maria Callas). Sometimes that's better, best, beyond technique. But I loved her young voice, which seemed not to tell the stories but to rise out of them.

*

I stayed up late to watch 'The Frankie Lyman Story'. As the credits roll at the end, the real Frankie Lyman suddenly appears in grainy black-and-white, rising, as if made of ash, out of postwar Ed Sullivan days, his voice careening through the changes of 'Goodie Goodie.' On the radio I'd thought it was Teresa Brewer, the voice like a woman's. But now I see it's Frankie Lyman, fourteen years old, conked and moon-faced, doing the splits, his disembodied silver voice gliding like a scalpel through the static of the 1950s.

*

I'm riding in the back seat of an old convertible, Greenwood district ca. 1959. Roy Orbison is on the radio, singing 'Only the Lonely', with some of Elvis's style but his voice vibrating in his head more than that; it was more like Buddy Holly's or Phil Everly's, but with more range than any popular singer of the time. That narcotically supple voice seemed to answer something or to something – the hatred directed toward rock from our parents' generation was not directed toward him.

Now someone is singing – a woman's voice or a child's? – down by the waves, near the ruin of Asbury Park – is it English? I know the melody but from where? I'll sit here, book open, unable to read, almost unable to see, the song blocking out my senses.

*

Three Poems

RACHEL HADAS

March Dawn

for Dawn Delbanco

Likelihood, luck, improvisation,
the meet-your-eye-in-the-mirror
epiphany. Spring opens up the sky:
more light, more space. But wait.
Bomb in the airport. Bomb on the subway.
In the market. In the playground.
Brussels. Lahore. No *but.* No *wait. And and:*
patient parataxis,
my teacher Robert Fagles used to say,
not hypotaxis. No subordination.
Homeric syntax was what he had in mind:
this and this and this and this.
Subway and airport and concert hall.
Blood and soft green spring.
Children at play and scattered limbs.
Or parataxis not so patient: life
improbably gifted, clutched
with abject gratitude. Why she, not you?
Why he or they, a horse, a rat, not I?
Trees in the park spread out their blurry fingers,
clutching at what? Warm spell;
this spring is early.
Blossoms on our magnolia ignite
The morning with their murderous five-days' white,
wrote Lowell, with more local dislocations

and threats in mind. Spring fangs.
Spring explosions. Safety?
Improbability of luck and grace,
oh take me home. But where is home, and what?
Home is the place where, when you have to go there,
They have to take you in,
wrote Frost. Presumably a place where strangers
cannot penetrate to do you harm.
Item: March dawn, wrote Merrill,
whose childhood home at 18 West 11th Street
was bombed by Weathermen,
spring 1970. *The siren drowns in choking smoke...*
Shards of a blackened witness still in place.
O deepening spring.
Home at last, you stretch. In a dawn dream
dark fingers surface and reach out for you.
Effortlessly one anxiety
fills the space vacated
by its predecessor.
These replacements last as long as life does.
Another hope, another victim,
Another death, another birth,
Another narrow, blessed, absurd escape.
Eyes in the mirror that you rise to face.
Home is the place.

The Garden: Boustrophedon, Enjambement, Repetition

Long lines. Somewhere a garden. Pass it on.
Boustrophedon, enjambement – repetition
however you deploy through space and time.
Green will recur,
an iron voice at the edge of sleep reminds me.
Green will keep coming back
only so long as you respect the rhythm:
change, fade, dwindle, wither, resurrect.
Keep by giving. Win by losing. Long
lines and repetition:
the garden sliding slowly out of sight
until it is a shimmering green hedge
seen out of the corner of the eye;
until it is the emblem of a law
I have been struggling to understand
all summer. All my life.

Gold lemon peach at dawn: tail of a dream
now rapidly retreating. Nothing new:
enjambement, repetition. Pass it on.
Awake, you pull the cord. Up goes the blind,
in comes another morning with its freight
of color and idea, and you go
out into a garden that's not yours,
or not yours only. Swallow that stern law.
Boustrophedon: the plow turns, so one furrow
runs east to west, the next one west to east.
Enjambement: straddle the little gap
left between lines-lines you have laid down
but have to leave for someone else to follow.
Vatic at dawn, the disembodied voice:
A garden, yes, but someone else's garden.
Yours? Yes, for the time being.
Yours to pass on. Theme and variation.
Boustrophedon, enjambement, repetition.

The Lost Pen

The prophetess in her dark cave.
How could I have failed to notice
order is an illusion?
Love's bubbling is part of the chaos.
To find oneself enmeshed in family,
the web of tangled lines, the thread pulled tight:
both our birthright and our final pattern,
comforting, predictable, random, hopeless.
Past or future? Patch it. Make it new
Until the next revision.
I've lost my favorite pen.
We stumble into the story in the middle.

Lit by the candle of complicated hope,
the stew of trouble simmers,
the barely lidded chaos.
Moonlight on snow: escape from day to dark.
Frozen landscape. Acreage for sale.
What I thought was mine is under threat,
not for the first time – it only feels that way.
A force field clouds drift over
until the next transformation:
incessant billowing, shrinkage, and revision.
Perhaps the pen has rolled under the table.
Close to the end – the end of what? Whose end?

The acolyte waits in the starlight.
I could catch planes on time, but where was I going?
Where was the anchor? There was no one to come
home to.
The time to pay the debt was running out.
Art off the walls! Let light have room to frolic.
Camel, weasel, whale, and the sky changes,
endless variation among the clouds,
pillows for sleep and dream without design.
I never found that pen, but took another,
As if writing it all down could make a difference.
Middle, beginning, end, all out of order.
Love works like that.

Orient und Okzident

BRIAN MORTON

Barbara Haus Schwepcke and Bill Swainson (editors), forewords by Daniel Barenboim
and Mariam C. Said, *A New Divan: A lyrical dialogue between East and West* (Ginkgo);
Marilyn Hacker, *Blazons: new and selected poems 2000–2018* (Carcanet)

'*ORIENT UND OKZIDENT / nicht mehr zu trennen.*' Even at the approaching end (surely?) of the jihadist spasm, even after a sturdy re-reading of Edward Said's *Orientalism*, which warned against reifying 'the East' as an exotic bazaar, Goethe's words might seem impossibly utopian, even as a wish. Kipling might seem to offer the more realistic prediction; the twain seem still reluctant to meet. Two centuries after Goethe mused on East and West, forty years after Said's salutary essay, the world is much foreshortened; Islam and what remains of Christendom are not so much in proximity as intermixed, but often not much better combined than oil and water and sometimes as binary explosive.

Goethe wrote his great *West-*ōstlicher *Divan* under the benign influence of the Persian pub poet Hafiz and in correspondence with his late love Marianne von Willemer; the wife of a friend, she became 'Suleika' to Goethe's 'Hatem', and may have contributed a couple of lovely lyrics to the East and West winds. In Weimar, Goethe's last home, there is a monument to the two (male) poets, a pair of chairs carved out of a single piece of granite and disposed facing one another in what still looks like an adversarial rather than companionable or clubby way, as if the world still doesn't quite know how to interpret Goethe's late masterpiece and its inspiration. And indeed, it remains surprisingly little known, continually 'rediscovered' and then left unread.

The world, when Goethe wrote it, was at war, in Europe but also in America, north and south. Exactly a century later, it was at war again, in what is usually taken, falsely, to be the 'first' world conflict. So imprinted are we with the paradigm of the Western Front that we now routinely forget that the First World War (which really was so labelled in 1914; 'Great War' might be better reserved for something else) was an episode in the continuing struggle of East and West, its Levantine theatre almost as strategically important as Verdun or Passchendaele. It has a Buchanish feel, this war; Buchan, like Kipling, had his faults, but he knew where the real 'Great War', logical extension of the 'Great Game', was to be waged.

Goethe, full in his years, preferred to think that cultural conflict could be reconciled. Twenty years ago – so many meaningful anniversaries! – a musical workshop was held in Weimar, 1999's Cultural Capital of Europe. Edward Said, Daniel Barenboim and cellist Yo Yo Ma were all present and the seeds of a multicultural ensemble were sown. The West-Eastern Divan Orchestra, heard at this year's Proms, was in the spirit of Goethe's poems, whose achievement, according to Said and quoted in the foreword to *A New Divan* by his widow Mariam, was the creation of 'an imaginative re-ordering of polarities, differences and opposition, on the basis not of politics but of affinities, spiritual generosity and aesthetic self-renewal'.

That is, of course, exactly what the *Divan,* and the engagement with Hafiz, had been for Goethe himself. 'Affinities' is a word we associate closely with him, because of *Wahlverwandtschaften*, the scientific novel of 1809 (which I also have in a translation called *Kindred By Choice*, an apposite title here!). *Faust Part One* had also just been published. But Goethe's romantic self-renewal was more fully expressed in verse and Hafiz gave him the freedom to do so.

The *West-*ōstlicher *Divan,* for all its grace and ease of reading, still somehow requires strenuous special pleading. Edward Dowden's 1914 translation seems almost ironically as well as obviously timed given what was happening in Europe, the Balkans and the Ottoman Empire. It had, in turn, depended on the first full translation of Hafiz by Joseph von Hammer, and it has depended since on scholarly imprimatur by Karl Krolow, pre-eminently by Katherina Mommsen in her *Goethe und der Islam*, and by Peter von Arnim, who died in 2009 before a new translation and meditation on the *Divan* could be published.

Gingko's *A New Divan* is not the first attempt to bring Goethe's vision up to date, but it is by far the boldest, drawing on the work of contemporary poets in German, Arabic, Spanish, Persian, Italian, French, Russian, Slovenian, Turkish, Portuguese, all presented with a facing English translation like the lobed gingko leaf that Goethe sent to Marianne as a sign of his/their, East's/West's 'one-yet-two' nature. It also provides the imprint with its name and colophon. Barbara Haus Schwepcke has also published a new set of 'inspirations' for the *Divan*, called *Hafiz, Goethe and the Gingko*, and a new annotated translation of the *Divan* itself by Eric Ormsby. Whether this latter supersedes the 2010 edition made by Martin Bidney, a senior comparative lettrist at Binghampton University, with the assistance of the late Peter von Arnim, is partly a matter of taste, though Bidney's introduction is valuable and von Arnim's translation of Goethe's contextual 'Notes and Essays' more than useful. What connects the two is that Bidney also writes his own series of poetic meditations on the themes and in the styles and rhythms of the *Divan*.

Those involved in the Gingko project include names that will be familiar to British readers, including Kathleen Jamie, Lavinia Greenlaw, Robin Robertson and Don Paterson, whose 'Eleven Maxims from the Book of Ill-Humour' is a highlight and delight: 'Read a poem slow enough / With vigilance and care / And you'll discover lots of stuff / that simply isn't there' is one to be pinned on the door of every postgrad lit. seminar in the Western world. More important than the thought, though, is the touch and feel. Goethe wrote with a gnomic ease only matched by his near-contemporary William Blake, an ability to combine simplicity and obscurity in a single trope, and to yoke together heterogeneous ideas *without* Metaphysical violence.

Genius nodding to genius, Heinrich Heine said that the defining quality of the *Divan* verses was that they were '*hingehaucht*' or 'naturally breathed'; they often expressed rude thoughts in quite ethereal terms, heretical ideas in ecstatic measures that accorded with Hafiz's exuberant acceptance of experience and Goethe's own Spinozan belief in nature as all-in-one. And this is very much the spirit of *A New Divan*. There is little of the familiar Coke-advert handholding in its poems, which are tough, sometimes irreverent, sometimes unexpectedly emotional, even sentimental, but driven along by rhythms and forms, especially that of the ghazal, that admit of no single dominating mood. Adonis's opening 'Letter to Goethe', beautifully translated from the Arabic by Khaled Mattawa, pretty much sums up the mood of the whole, though only a re-reading delivers its quiet smile: 'The West is behind you, but the East is not before me. // They are two banks of one river.' Sisyphus, Sinbad, Gilgamesh and Ulysses are all invoked before: 'One body is ripped limb by limb: / A body that has no East except its name, / A body that has no West except its name.' Even the seeming idiomatic lapse – 'limb *from* limb' is more usual – seems to work here, as does the rapid shuttering between time-frames. Abbas Beydoun does this even more boldly, putting Suleika/Marianne in the same Gaze as tragic Marilyn Monroe and in the process calling not just on Hafiz but on Saadi, Rumi, Mutanabbi as well.

Djinns and alembics put in an appearance in other poems, as does Auschwitz. Much more than Bidney's more obviously lyrical approach, the Gingko poets seem to use the *Divan* not as a bustling street market of imagery but as a lens to look at our times. Perhaps the most remarkable poem of the set, and one of the most strangely beautiful, is Hafez Mousavi's 'The Name of that Sad Dove', translated by Alireza Abiz and Daisy Fried, which seems to bring together Baucis and Philemon (a Darby and Joan who fed the gods) with a modern airstrike, Goethe's friend Schiller with the now-threatened EU project whose anthem is his (and Beethoven's) '*An die Freude/Ode to Joy*', Silesian weavers with Rilke's panther. It's a virtuosic performance that doesn't dwell on its own virtuosity and which even in its more arresting moments ('the black milk of morning') seems conversational and companionable rather than 'poetic'. Let that stand for *A New Divan* as a whole, but it is as a whole that it needs to be read, a new single poem rather than an anthology, the work of a collective voice, respectful of Goethe but prepared to use his optics rather than merely paying homage.

The *West-östlicher Divan* is unmistakably a work of maturity. The young never evince so much ease. In an introduction to the 1914 Dowden translation, 'E.D.D.' – presumably his second wife and widow Elizabeth Dickinson Dowden – says of it that it represents 'Goethe's Indian summer of art-life', and for once that over-used colonial description makes perfect sense. She spoils it a little with a reference to 'sexagenarian love-making', but there it is. It's exactly the mood one senses in Marilyn

Hacker's wonderful new collection, also the product of an Indian summer of poetic life. *Blazons* consists of new poems, more translations from the Arabic and French (work for which she has been rightly feted), and a set of Apollinaire-like 'Calligraphies', some of which have appeared already in *PNR* [*PN Review*]. There is boldness as well as ease – this is the word we're going to have to rely on – in all these poems. Hacker has lived for the last ten years in Paris and 'Itinerants' is a sequence of Paris street-scenes, some painted by Utrillo, some acted out by the Mme Hulot we always wanted to see in a starring role, some driven by the not-forgotten spirit of 1968. Hacker weaves together imagistic glimpses with an ongoing story about an HIV half-way house and the campaign against it. She observes the passing show and the wider narrative provided over coffee by *Le Monde*. 'Place des Vosges: October' is a gloriously autumnal perspective on how time and memory and how the years betray. In reply a friend interjects, changing the whole tone of the poem in the way Goethe's occasional irruptions of violence do, 'Your friend says, 'Turncoats sell their arse to the flies / and then complains that history is unjust'.' Hacker gets the killer last line with 'For a breath of paradox, you are in the present.'

And so she is. Admittedly, helped with Migralgine. She doesn't shrink from a brand name here and there, any more than she shrinks from scientific jargons: 'butyls and titrans' appear in one of the 'Calligraphies', aromatic canisters jostling with winejars, a Goethean touch, perhaps. And she has never, throughout her career, shrunk from the particulars of love-making, sexagenarian or otherwise. In the title poem, 'Blazons', perhaps the most virtuosic musical poetry she has ever composed and the most visually intense, there is a reference to 'Suspicion of the hooded clitoris' (repeated twice as the end/beginning of two stanzas) and to a memory, someone's, of multiple orgasms. She does the same thing, though, with the 'irrelevant' detail of 'a scimitar of scar across her chest', which suggests mastectomy but also transports us East and the cruelties of Timur Lenk which hover behind the *Divan.* The repeated line prompts an entirely contingent echo of one of Paterson's cheerfully grim saws in his 'Book of Ill-Humour': 'Don't forget her, son, / heartbroken as you are; it's a waste of a good wound / to heal without a scar'. Dundee meets Kesh: embraces.

Throughout her career Hacker has shown a gift, instinctive but evolving, for form. It's there in *Essays on Departure*, an earlier Carcanet collection, but it has refined and extended in *Blazons*, which includes sonnets, villanelle-like Malay pantoums, ghazals and tankas, which are less celebrated than haiku and with a looser beat. Nothing exposes a 'Western' artist more than dabbling in 'Eastern' forms, but Hacker's ghazals entirely lack the unconvincing twangs of 'ethnic' music that routinely accompany tv shots of Taj Mahal, pagoda or Eiffel Tower. There is, so to speak, no accordion music in her Paris street scenes. Instead, they are robustly multi-ethnic, mingled if not always harmonious. They're also comfortable with the banal, which may also conceal something more sinister like the cops waiting across the street, or the immigrant woman who may look calm, bored, stoical but who haven't forgotten dead babies left behind.

'Ghazal: Across the Street' engages more closely than any other poem with the question of who 'you' refers to. At times it appears to be Hacker; at times, an unnamed or –identified (but not always silent) interlocutor; at times, it can only be us. Which is why, when she begins another ghazal 'Unmistakable, that consummate style / pierces the incoherence of her late style', we can only nod and agree. Unmistakable, yes; consummate, absolutely; incoherent, only in the sense that experience is loosely woven and not fused. We need to remember that the derivation of ghazal isn't just spooning and sweet-talking, isn't just about the pangs of love, but also relates to spinning yarn. Nobody spins a poetic yarn more convincingly than Marilyn Hacker, even if the narrative is only glimpsed through the slats of a blind and all dazzle beyond it.

It is perhaps remarkable, and perhaps not, that a child of the Bronx, who attended its High School of Science (other notable alumni include [critic] Harold Bloom, [novelists] E.L. Doctorow and Richard Price, latter-day bard Peter S. Beagle, and Hacker's former husband Samuel R. Delany) should have acquired such a capacious vision. Perhaps only a young woman schooled in Bronx Sci's brand of metrics could come to show such ease with metrics of another sort. There isn't a false note here, even when the literal meaning isn't manifest. The translations, whether from Arabic or French, seem to inhabit a place between 'literal' and 'poetic', roles very often assigned to different voices in *A New Divan*.

Both books succeed only because they press back against the current xenophobia as stoutly as Goethe tried to ignore it in 1814. Something of the sci fi strangeness she explored with Delany persists in Hacker's work, but with the clear implication that 'alien' is an extremely relative term, which has metaphysical as well as legal implications. 'Orient and Occident / Cannot be parted for ever more.' Perhaps not. 'Orientalism' still persists, but it's a happy occident that these two remarkable books should emerge together in this dangerous summer.

A Tourniquet for Emily Davison

SINÉAD MORRISSEY

I found her listed under Flora
Smudged on a coloured, shining plate
Dogeared and dirty. As for Fauna
We are all that, pelted with anarchy.
W.S. GRAHAM

A harridan-Houdini, cages – and not just the ribcage of that final horse
you hailed like a tram on Tattenham Corner – *they the reynes*
of his brydel henten – but corsets, railings, handcuffs, cubby holes,
heat shafts inside the Houses of Parliament, taunted you all your life,
faire Emelye, like the Keep Out signs on the King's Estate
or the clang of your yellowing cell in Strangeways
each time they frogmarched you back. What manner of woman *were* you?
Appalled editorials harrumphed in a fug of pipe fumes;
a child on a poster in a nacreous cardigan wept stunted tears of neglect –
Mummy's a Suffragette! – outside Marylebone Station.

At first the slippery trick of fasting set you free, by which the bones
assert their own supremacy: your sentences axed repeatedly
just by turning the face of Kafka's Hunger Artist or a starveling Christ
before Pentecost towards your captors. Queasiness in Whitehall;
a burn like caustic soda through the notion of *gentleman.*
But it didn't take long for the State to stiffen its spine, roll up its sleeves
and conjure a bag of tricks of its own: a tube, a buckle, a funnel, a gag,
your own body breathing on its slab, forced to outfox you.
You staggered from each feeding session dishevelled and drenched,
a veteran of rough seas and shipwrecks.

It must have been dizzying, the *tableau vivant* of each arrest so grimly
asymmetrical: whatever cry for justice launched towards man and heaven,
whatever momentary, public flurry – exploding glass, fire in a pillar box –
collapsed suddenly to a woman with her hair undone, pale as a peony,
pinned between policemen. Horses, compacted torsos
and high-stepping hooves, flanked you here also:
their sinews the sinews of the immutable world, viciously reasserted.
As rain continued to fall on the reasonable cobblestones
you were escorted away from the theatre of the street like an apostate
over and over again, in violet weathers.

Buoyed, maverick, hooked – *through my humble work* –
already by 1909 you could never be bound by the epithets
found on most women's headstones. From letters to newspapers
to stones to horsewhips to dropping yourself from a balcony –
if Calvary haunted you, it was Calvary garlanded
with Deeds Not Words, white dresses fluttering from its Crosses.
But the century, as well as your life, was speeding up –
portraits of nothing and very like, tinted steam –
cast back at its witnesses as jittery footage. So as the 8.15
from Victoria bore south through the shuttered villages

and children stood to watch it pass as always and a slack mist
lay on the fields and London was emptied of bookies and flower sellers
and motor cars stalled at the gates and women in hats like avalanches
chatted and laughed – little heartflowers, little emptinesses,
bubbles in the blood cascading upwards –
you fingered the stub in your pocket, the scarf at your throat
and the train dispatched its smoke and the crowd surged high
as a wave and set you down on time and the guard rail snickered.
Then your ashen flash and fall so fast the newsreel almost missed it –
the dynamite of the tenth of a second – then nothing.

Rain Clouds and other poems

N I N A   B O G I N

Rain Clouds

Rain clouds as they descend
over the hills, ragged

and somber,
make a kind of home

in the valley below.
Like a roof over a house

where a fire is burning
in the hearth

for someone who comes in
from the rain.

Or like our marriage –
year after year together

in the shelter of the foothills.

Rain sweeps across the road,
lifting branches, scattering leaves –

the end of summer.
It's only later, afterwards,

that we recognize happiness
for what it was.

Old House

Long abandoned, it leans back
from the road, its roof aslant.

The rosebush with pink roses
that pleased a farmer

or a farmer's wife
still climbs beside the doorway.

Once I glimpsed a woman there,
a widow perhaps, with her son.

They must have cleared the yard
one last time, taken

the crocheted cushions,
the crockery, the rocking chair...

The garden fills up with weeds.
The gate is rusted shut.

Should we not try to be
as brave as that house

with its white-framed windows
and worn sandstone stoop,

with stars spilling through the roof?

Swatch

I won't wear it.
It ticks silently in my handbag,
deep inside a pocket.

A man's watch, with a thick black
watchband only a man would wear.
Now it's a keepsake,

half-forgotten.
Today, belatedly, I changed
the hour to daylight saving.

Time goes backwards
as well as forward.
A year ago you laughed

at our old jokes,
sang your favorite songs.
In the last weeks

everything was clear
and white – the hospital room
in August light, the air

on our skin.
I drove back and forth.
My time was fastened

to yours, like a watch
around a wrist, those days
of words and touch

when unaccountably
you were yourself again.

Letter in May

You'd be surprised to learn
I live alongside a river

in a pale-pink house you never got to see,
with windowsills and flower pots

and an iron fence painted periwinkle-blue.
Today the wind is banging

neighbors' shutters and garden gates,
a cold springtime wind

sweeping in from the east
with apple blossoms and the smell

of freshly baked bread, exhaust fumes, lilacs...
Yesterday I walked along the river

with a friend. The sky was bluer
than it's been for months

and the town, that I always thought drab,
washed by a week of rain

flaunted its muted colors – rose sandstone,
ochre – in an excess of light.

You should know, as promised,
I've planted a flowering plum tree

in a corner of the garden, adding the last
of your ashes to the earth around the roots,

tamping down the soil for the tree
to take hold. A closing act

in this season of renewal?
I can't say.

And if I'm typing slowly
with the three middle fingers of my right hand

it's because our cat is sprawled
across my left arm, and you know

how I hate to disturb her.

'The simple arithmetic of brutality'

David Herman

Alexandra Popoff, *Vasily Grossman and the Soviet Century* (Yale University Press) £25
Vasily Grossman, *Stalingrad*, translated by Robert and Elizabeth Chandler (Harvill Secker) £25
John & Carol Garrard, *The Life and Fate of Vasily Grossman* (Pen & Sword Military) £25

ON 14 FEBRUARY 1961 three KGB officers entered Vasily Grossman's apartment in Moscow and confiscated more than 10,000 pages of typescripts, including seven drafts of Grossman's masterpiece, *Life and Fate*, one of the greatest novels of the twentieth century.

Grossman was an outstanding war novelist and reporter. From 1941–45 he was attached to the Red Army. He wrote about two of the bloodiest battles of the Second World War, Stalingrad and Kursk, the greatest tank battle in history.

Grossman was also among the first to write about the Holocaust. As the Germans retreated, he saw what had happened to the Jews in the Ukraine and wrote his famous report, 'Ukraine without Jews' (unpublished in Russian during his lifetime). His mother was one of 12,000 Jews killed in one day at Berdichev, one of the first mass killings by the *Einsatzgruppen*. *He never recovered from her death. As he continued west with the Red Army in 1944, Grossman entered Poland. In September they arrived at Treblinka. His report, 'The Hell of Treblinka', was one of the first published accounts of a Nazi death camp. It was widely translated and distributed at Nuremberg as part of the evidence against the Nazis. He brought back a child's building block and a shoe from Treblinka. He continued to Berlin and saw the Imperial Reich Chancellery. 'Hitler's armchair and table,' he wrote. 'A huge metal globe, crushed and flattened.'*

Above all, however, Grossman was one of the great chroniclers of Stalinism. In the short stories in *The Road* and in his novels, he described the Gulag, collectivization and famine and the atmosphere of terror under Stalin. His courage was extraordinary. When his second wife was arrested in 1938, he wrote to Yezhov, asking for her case to be reviewed. As Popoff points out, this was like 'putting his own head in a noose.' He was summoned to the Lubyanka. He survived and she was soon released.

On 2 May 1990, as the Soviet regime was rocking, Fyodor Burlatsky, chief editor of the leading literary weekly *Literaturnaya gazeta*, wrote that the most important precursors of the changes sweeping Soviet society under Gorbachev were 'Khruschev's report on Stalin's crimes at the twentieth Party Congress, Solzhenitsyn's *One Day in the Life of Ivan Denisovich*, and Grossman's *Life and Fate*.'

Grossman was born in Berdichev in the Ukraine in 1905. He was one of the youngest members of that extraordinary generation of Jewish writers born in the Russian Empire, who lived through the Stalin years, and which included Isaac Babel, Boris Pasternak, Yevgenia Ginzburg, Osip and Nadezhda Mandelstam. It is no coincidence that many of these wrote some of the classic accounts of Stalinism.

'Berdichev,' write the Garrards, 'was the thread that knit all the tangles of Grossman's life. His first extensive article was "Berdichev for Real – No Kidding", published in 1929. His first piece of fiction, published in 1934, was also set in Berdichev.' A decade later he wrote, 'The Murder of the Jews of Berdichev' for *The Black Book*.

Berdichev was home to one of Europe's largest Jewish communities. At one time the town had eighty synagogues. In 1897, a few years before Grossman was born, the population of Berdichev was just over 50,000. 41,000 were Jews.

Grossman was born Iosif Solomonovich Grossman but later adopted the name, Vasily. It was more Russian and, crucially, less Jewish. He was born into an emancipated and educated Jewish family. 'We were not like the poor shtetl Jews described by Sholem Aleichem,' he wrote later to his daughter. His parents were both from the professional upper middle class, assimilated, Europeanised. They spoke Russian and French not Yiddish. Families like the Grossmans were a minority within a minority, neither Ukrainians, nor *stetl* Jews, who were mostly religious, poor and Yiddish-speaking.

From the beginning he was an outsider. Brought up without a father, living with his mother on the charity of wealthy relatives and Jewish, at a time when during the Russian Civil War there were 1200 pogroms in Ukraine.

He studied chemistry in Moscow during the 1920s, married briefly, and published his first newspaper articles. In the early 1930s he started writing, producing his first novel and between 1935 and 1937 he published three books of short stories. He caught the eye of significant figures like Gorky and Bulgakov.

Grossman survived the *Yezhovschina*, the Stalinist Terror in the late 1930s. Some of his closest friends, however, were arrested and shot. His second wife was briefly arrested and his uncle David, who had supported Grossman and his mother during his childhood, was arrested, presumed shot. One cousin was arrested and never heard from again. Another was arrested, deported to Astrakhan. She was subsequently rearrested and sent to a labour camp in Siberia for three more years.

The real turning point in Grossman's life came in 1941. First, he became a frontline war reporter for the popular Red Army newspaper, *Krasnaya Zvezda* (Red Star), spending more than 1,000 days covering the Eastern Front, from the Battle of Moscow and Stalingrad to the Battle of Berlin. Sir Antony Beevor, who edited a selection of Grossman's war journalism, called Grossman, 'the most perceptive and honest eyewitness of the Soviet frontlines between 1941 and 1945'.

Grossman developed an enormous admiration for the courage and tough life of ordinary Soviet soldiers, often fighting against overwhelming odds under appalling conditions. 'In battle,' he wrote, 'the Russian dons a white shirt. He may live a sinful life, but he dies like a saint. At the front many Russians have a purity of thought and soul, a kind of monk-like modesty.'

What is striking here is the Christian imagery. Two of the greatest accounts of war in the twentieth century were Isaac Babel's Red Cavalry and Grossman's war reports, two bespectacled Jews travelling with antisemitic Cossacks on the one hand and antisemitic Soviet soldiers on the other. Their situation as Jews is not trivial or accidental. It is where much of the moral complexity of their writing comes from.

The war marked a shift in Grossman's writing from the socialist realism of his first novel in the 1930s to the extraordinary writing of the 1940s and '50s. There is the unblinking gaze at the inhumanity of war. Grossman, write the Garrards, noted the deliberate policy of the Germans to deprive Soviet POWs of food and medical assistance: 'This act of gross inhumanity condemned men whose faces had been blistered off by flamethrowers to an agonizing death, with no analgesics to ease the pain... As the war went on, the Wehrmacht began routinely to strip captured Red Army soldiers of their warm greatcoats, hats, and felt boots... in the process condemning men to death by freezing.'

He wrote of young women who deliberately wore rags and rubbed ashes on their faces to make themselves unattractive so they might not be raped by German soldiers. He wrote of how Russian soldiers cut the legs off frozen German bodies and thawed them on the stove so it was easier to remove the boots. Sometimes they used the frozen legs for fuel.

The war didn't just teach Grossman how to write. It taught him about the nature of Stalinism: the ruthlessness of Stalin's 'Not One Step Back!' order of 28 July 1942; the decision to call Soviet POWs 'traitors to the Motherland'; denying that Ukrainian and Belorussian POWs had collaborated with the Germans; the refusal to acknowledge the Holocaust (the so-called policy of 'Do not divide the dead'); the lack of Soviet preparedness at the time of the German invasion which led the criminal sacrifice of millions of Soviet soldiers. Grossman witnessed all this and knew that the state lied again and again about what really happened during the war.

The second life-changing event of these years was the Holocaust, in particular, the massacre at Berdichev, according to the Garrards, 'the largest mass shooting of Jews ever undertaken until that time'. Just a few days later the killers at Berdichev shot more than 30,000 Jews at Babi Yar.

As they liberated the Ukraine, The Red Army discovered the mass graves of hundreds of thousands of Jews. 'There are no Jews in Ukraine,' he wrote. 'Nowhere... All is silence. Everything is still. A whole people have been brutally murdered.' He also wrote, 'The Old Schoolteacher', a story about the events leading up to the shooting of hundreds of Jews in a small Ukrainian town. At one pojnt, the teacher says, 'It's simple arithmetic – the simple arithmetic of brutality.' Few writers knew this arithmetic better than Grossman. 'Taken together,' write the Garrrards, 'Grossman's two pieces are the first treatments anywhere, fictional or documentary, in any language, of what was later known as the Holocaust.'

Grossman witnessed dozens of interrogations of captured Nazis. 'Not once,' he wrote, 'have I observed remorse, horror, despair...' He learned the details of mass executions. For 'an experienced organizer', one said, it should take two and a half hours to kill a thousand people. The execution squad doesn't need to be big – 'not more than twenty men for a thousand Jews.' Grossman wrote of mass graves where women and children had been buried alive – 'forensic anatomists found sand in their lungs.'

The Life and Fate of Vasily Grossman by John and Carol Garrard, begins with the atrocity at Berdichev and at least one hundred pages of the book is about the Holocaust. It is arguably the moral centre of their book.

Alexandra Popoff's book is more political and literary. She has written a number of books on other Russian writers and illuminates Grossman's life story with fascinating references to Soviet authors, from Bulgakov and Mandelstam in the 1930s to Grossman's friend Ilya Ehrenberg. Her biography comes to life with the post-war years, with Grossman's battle to publish his last great novels, *Life and Fate*, *Everything Flows* and *Stalingrad*.

Popoff's great advantage over the Garrards is that she is coming to the subject more than twenty years later. Their biography was first published as *The Bones of Berdichev* in 1996, and though a second edition was published in 2012, with a new title, nothing in the Bibliography was published after the mid-90s. There has been a huge historiographical revolution since then. Historians like Anne Appelbaum, Timothy Snyder and Steven Kotkin have radically reshaped the way we think about Stalinism.

Also during these years, a number of key figures from Grossman's life have published their memoirs, in particular, Alexander Tvardovsky, chief editor of the highly influential literary magazine, *Novy mir*, in the 1950s and early '60s. Tvardovsky, Aleksandr Fadeyev, general secretary of the Writers Union for almost twenty years, and Konstantin Simonov, chief editor of *Novy mir* until 1950, were significant figures. They decided whether Grossman got published or not. Two of his major novels, *Life and Fate* and *Everything Flows*, did not appear in Russian until *glasnost*. Even when they agreed to publish him, they cut it till it was unrecognisable. In the words of Grossman's friend, Anna Berzer, he was 'buried alive'.

These editors were hugely important but they are all marginal in the Garrards' biography. Just eleven references to Tvardovsky, nine to Fadeyev, eight to Simonov. Popoff, by contrast, writes movingly and in great detail about Grossman's battle with the *apparatchiks*. It is the best part of her book.

The Garrards and Popoff are good on the life and the historical and cultural context. But they are less good on what makes Grossman such an extraordinary writer. They don't pick up on the key literary influences, the recurring themes and images. For example, Isaac Babel was clearly an important influence on 'In the Town of Berdichev', just as Tolstoy is a huge influence on *Life and Fate and Stalingrad*. *'During the whole war,'* Grossman wrote later, *'the only book that I read was War and Peace which I read twice.' It is surely no coincidence that in October 1941, in the midst of the chaos of the German invasion, Grossman visited Tolstoy's House at Yasnaya Polyana.*

Good biographers, they are not at their best as critics. For example, how often Grossman's central characters are alone and isolated. 'No one else truly kept him in mind,' the narrator says in his story, *The Elk*. When Anna Borisovna Lomova, the tragic widow in his story, 'Living Space', dies, 'Nobody attended her cremation.' She was neglected by everyone else while she was alive and cruelly ignored after she died. In his novel, *Everything Flows*, he writes of a character returning from the camps, 'The loneliness he felt when he awoke was so total that it seemed to him more than any creature on earth, any air-breathing creature, could survive.' Characters in the great novels are constantly separated from their families or loved ones.

Most isolated of all are the children and orphans in Grossman's writing: Alyosha's abandoned child in his story, 'In The Town of Berdichev', the childless couple and orphan in 'A Small Life', and, most movingly of all, the orphan girl in 'Mama'.

What kind of writer was Grossman? Curiously old-fashioned in some ways. There is an extraordinary passage in *Stalingrad*:

> When people read obscure novels, when they listen to over-complex music or look at a frighteningly unintelligible painting, they feel anxious and unhappy. The thoughts and feelings of the novel's characters, the sounds of the symphony, the colours of the painting – everything seems peculiar and difficult., as if from some other world...
>
> But there are also books that make a reader exclaim joyfully, 'Yes, that's just what *I* feel. I've gone through that to and that's what I thought myself.'
>
> Art of this kind does not separate people from the world. Art like this connects people to life, to other people and to the world as a whole. It does not scrutinize life through strangely tinted spectacles.
>
> As they read this kind of book, people feel that they are being infused with life, that the vastness and complexity of human existence is entering into their blood, into the way they think and breathe.
>
> [...] In this clear, calm and deep simplicity lies the truth of genuine art.

This is extraordinary in so many ways. It is as if the author suddenly steps forward to address the reader directly. But, above all, it is wonderfully old-fashioned, as if almost fifty years of Literary Theory had never happened. All this talk of what readers 'feel' and how art 'connects people to life'. It makes us think of a debate that hasn't really happened but perhaps should. A debate not about Modernism or Post-Modernism, but another kind of tradition altogether. Writers like Orwell and Koestler, Levi and Wiesel, Grossman and Pasternak who wrote clearly and simply about terrible things that were done to people in the mid-twentieth century.

There are many examples of this kind of plain writing in *Stalingrad*. Chapter 21 describes the first night of the war on the Eastern Front, 22 June 1941. It begins, 'Novikov was always able to recall the first night of the war with absolute clarity.' Such clear, simple prose.

A few pages into the chapter on the first night of the war, Novikov, a key figure in the novel, 'went to the grand, spacious dining room.' '[A] plentiful meal [is] put in front of him: meat patties and fried potatoes in an enamel bowl, followed by thin pancakes with sour cream on a gilt-rimmed porcelain plate with a picture of a shepherdess in a pink dress, surrounded by white sheep.'

In a way this is simple and old-fashioned descriptive writing. But this short passage does something else. It reminds us of many meals in *Stalingrad*. Very early on, in Chapter 5, Vavilov is about to go off to war. He sits at his table: 'On it stood a bowl of potatoes, a saucer with a little white, crystallized honey, some slices of bread ands a mug of milk. He ate slowly.' Again, such simple food. Like the simple prose. But as we read other accounts of food, we realise that often these meals take place in poor peasant homes, like Vavilov's. This traditional food and the pastoral imagery ('a shepherdess in a pink dress') is reassuring, safe, in contrast to the chaos and mayhem that runs through the book. It also rubs up against the new Soviet society that is emerging in the novel: 'A whole new panoply of professions had been born: industrial and agricultural planners, peasant scientists, beekeeper scientists, cattle breeders, vegetable growers, kolkhoz engineers, radio operators, tractor drivers, electricians. Russia had attained an unprecedented level of literacy and general enlightenment, a sudden leap whose power can be compared only with that of some cosmic force...'

This is a thrilling evocation of the new Soviet Union. No shepherdesses here. And, of course, no peasants. Because as Grossman knew better than anyone, peasants had been starved in their millions and those who weren't starved to death had been shot or deported to the east. Those meals start to feel more charged.

This is one chain of images about food and meals which take us in so many directions which are not at all clear or simple. Another chain, this time about homes, appears at the end of this chapter about Novikov and the beginning of the war:

> His country seemed to him like a single huge house, and everything in this house was infinitely dear to him: small whitewashed rooms in villages, rooms in towns and cities, with colourful lampshades; quiet reading rooms; brightly lit halls; the Red Corners of army barracks.

You think of all the houses and homes in *Stalingrad* and how many of the central characters are driven from their homes. Some return, some don't. So many of the most moving scenes in the novel are about returning home. Viktor Shtrum returns to his Moscow apartment ('The apartment had barely changed since the day they left... Everything was as it always had been – yet also, somehow, unfamiliar and strange.')

Almost 130 pages later, Viktor returns to his *dacha*: 'Finally, he was able to unlock the door. The orderly appearance of his untouched room was somehow more startling than the chaos elsewhere; it was as if only a week had passed since that last Sunday before the war.'

This constant movement between being driven from homes and returning home runs through the novel. It gives *Stalingrad* its extraordinary sense of movement, as if the whole country – peasants, physicists, nurses – had just been tipped up and landed just anywhere, from Stalingrad to Kazan.

Something else happens in Viktor's *dacha*. He sees that 'his unread manuscript still lay on the floor, close to the bed'. But this isn't the only manuscript. In his briefcase, Viktor finds 'a small package and thought it was a bar of chocolate he had brought for Nina. Then he remembered it had been given to him by Novikov.' He opens the package: 'Viktor sat down and glanced through the long letter.

It was his mother's record of her last days – from the beginning of the war until the eve of her inevitable death behind the barbed wire of the Jewish ghetto. It was her farewell to her son.'

The letter from Anna Semyonovna to her son is passed from hand to hand seven times in *Stalingrad* and we don't read it until we read the sequel, *Life and Fate*. The adventures of this letter are like something from *Tristram Shandy* or Derrida's reading of Lacan's reading of Poe's *Purloined Letter*. This fascination with a text that keeps vanishing and is never read is not at all like 'the clear, calm and deep simplicity' that Grossman wrote about in that great passage about literature. And as we reflect on this, we realise that Grossman is not interested in either simple, clear storytelling or the strange adventures of a manuscript that never gets read. He offers us both, just as he offers us the shepherdess *and* the starving peasants, calm and silence but also devastation and bloodshed.

And then there is Tolstoy's home. In Chapter 50, Krymov, another central character in both *Stalingrad* and *Life and Fate*, stops off at Yasnaya Polyana, where Tolstoy wrote, *War and Peace*. Krymov has been here before:

But when he went inside this second time, Krymov felt that this was a Russian house like any other. The storm that had flung open every door in Russia, that had driven people out of their warm homes and onto black autumn roads, sparing neither peaceful city apartments, nor village hits, nor hamlets deep in the forest, had treated Leo Tolstoy's home no less harshly... Yasnaya Polyana was a living, suffering Russian home – one of thousand upon thousand of such homes. With absolute clarity, Krymov saw in his mind Bald Hills and the old, sick prince.

That word 'clarity' again. It is no accident that Krymov visits Tolstoy's home. Nothing transparent or simple about that choice. More interesting, though, is something else that Grossman does again and again in *Stalingrad*. One minute you are close up, looking at the telling detail: the shepherdess, the manuscript that looks like a chocolate bar. And then he pulls out and he has suddenly 'flung open every door in Russia', and you see a whole society on the move. This is what *Stalingrad* does all the time. Grossman talks about 'deep simplicity' but his writing is anything but simple.

Neither the Garrards or Popoff read Grossman's writing with great attention to detail. But they do offer something else. They bring his times to life. There is no jargon. They write clearly and well. They have done their research, gone to archives, interviewed people who knew him. These are both fine biographies, passionate and erudite. Above all, they never lose sight of the darkness of these times, the terrible moral choices. Do you risk everything by going to the Lubyanka to try and save your wife? Do you dare criticise the regime? Do you write to Stalin to try and get your life works published?

These biographies should be read beside *Stalingrad*. What emerges from these three books is a new sense of Grossman's life but, above all, the conviction that he was one of the great writers of the twentieth century.

---

softboi season and other poems

ANNIE FAN

---

softboi season

oxford, 2019

o lesser cousin of the fuckboi, less likely a rower; o one who wears unwashed jumpers and mangles proust, cries into his cosmos and parades shorts even in december. i saw one of you coming down on high street, socks and sliders (both of which your breed have mansplained to me); and another nearly ran me over, bike basket filled with apollinaire and adorno, didn't ring but sang an aria in warning; i nearly died. tell me why i can't seem to shake the bad poets and wine boys, can't find a single specimen who doesn't play jazz to his cats at night or drinks in graveyards. even the physics boys! have taken up their austen and keats, have defied their classification, declaim historiographic metafiction from their labs, vibration/communication. yes; let me live free of mahler, liccs and bad kisses; your opinion pieces and union speeches; o all unfaithful vegans and vegetarians; can i say; enough?

Sonnet Which Is Not a Sonnet

oh oxford and your distinct lack
of chinatowns, your soggy stone
mornings and such english breakfasts,
the distinct lack of food other than
breakfast on weekends, lack of
sun, insulation, edible dumplings;
give me neon-glare, greenlit
sushi places, low-calorie, calorie-free
asian noodles; what can be more
asian than a noodle, more asian
than me; I – who cannot read
the chinese newsletter, the chinese
buildings, who only understand food
and lack, this lack of edible china,
the only kind of language, chinese
language, I have, fully fluent?

Ode to a Wound

supposing, instead / that it was not the
end of things, that it was not supposed
to be a means to circle the wild thing
with ash, to tame it and tame itself
out of it, it. it followed me back home
and stomped about in its dark, plastic boots
shaking the whole foundation apart from
its roots – a chasm afloat in something
like winter, thick enough for stirring by
spoon. it told me to eat, and I sipped
the blood off the water; to lick and I
played dead by the river, hiding under
the stones. each season has its own kind
of animal. and it was there, it knew
all the crawlspaces – that only night could
bloom wild, perfect things. much later,
autumn sends it seeping back into my
throat, its hands, everywhere at once
inside the careful loops of a handknitted
scarf, its prayers struck into even the grey
sponge inside bones; it the maker,
it the body, beyond / myself, the river
of all rivers, the sea, the sea, a stoning.

Martial

DUNCAN WU

Issa the Pisser

Martial, Epigrams *1.109*

Who scraps harder than Catullus's badass
Sparrow? Who's purer than Milton's impreg-
nating dove, hotter than the Flying
Scorpion, pole-riding Empress of Lap-
land, swankier than a facefull of
The wildest beluga caviar? Yes,
Issa, that darling lapdog of Publius.
She yelps with the acid tongue of silver-
Palated Demosthenes on the
Humiliations and ecstasies of
The canine condition. And when she needs
A piss, lovely Issa, the sheets remain spotless;
She raises her snout from her pillow, gazes
Deep in his eyes, scrapes his cheek with her
Crusty pawpads, and croons. What a bitch!
What a lady! What a gal! As modest,
Becoming, and virtuous as a nun,
The demure canine debutante tucks her tail
Round her privates, snarls at the sausage-hounds
And growls from the depths of her guts – faithful
Only to her Publius.

Besotted,
He yearns never to lose her, so creates
Her hologram, her mnemonic, her specter,
Closer to Issa than Issa herself.
It wolfs down its supper, then passes gas,
It pants and it drools, it eats its own ass
And consumes his soul. Eyes only for it,
He casts off the real thing, locks her out of
The house, surrendering instead to her
Icon. It compels, it enchants, it leads
Him a dance, it fills him with bright shining
Light; it feasts on his liver, sucks his brains
From his nose, drains his white blood cells right out of
His toes.
            Next day comes Carmen, his
Filippino factotum, who finds his corpse
Crumpled in on itself, a crispy husk
Of dried-out, brittle, inert human crackling,
While the mechanic image of Issa
Squats over him, snuffles, squitters and snorts.
It wolfs down its supper, then passes gas,
It pants and it drools, it eats its own ass.

Temptation

Martial, Epigrams *9.41*

So, Anthony, you think it doesn't matter,
That you don't, won't, or can't make ravage,
When in the bedroom you do not savage,
That you prefer that simian grip, that
Darwinian slip, an obsidian
Whip, to any woman? Yet must the world be
Peopled. Only once did Frank pizzle in
Olivia for her to beget triplets;
Mark gave Margot the rampant horse-shunting
Required to give her quins. Had either spizzed
Off like you, none of that would have happened,
And their crib giblets, those squib midgets, would
Not exist. You see, your asex-naysex
Is irrationality, half-way down
The road to insubstantiality,
Redolent of a sociopathic
Personality. See? Your fallacy
Masturbatory, your phone-in to Onan,
Your self-detonating pipe-bomb, your
D.I.Y. pogrom, is outragement, self-
Estrangement, genital disarrangement –
In short, mass-murder. And at what cost to
You, this delusional disorder? Brisk
Downgrade of bodily fibers and organs,
Heightened susceptibility to
Gonorrheal rhinitis, venereal
Gingivitis, syphilitic diarrhea;
Need I say more? Deviant dermatitis,
Paranoid prostatitis, psychotic
Sinusitis, maniacal mastitis,
Schizoid cellulitis, the dance of St
Vitus; deflationary dysentery,
Testy-zesty epilepsy, baldness,
Blackheads, galloping bum-fluff, bunions,
Bedbugs and crill.
                        Who advances towards
Us? A young man with a walking-stick; hear
Him squeak and gibber like one of the damned
As they limp their way to the technicolor
Trauma of the fiery fuckpit. Fie fie
Fie the fiery fuckpit, out of which armpit
We forge that obit. Nor is he alone,
Can you see them advancing? That woman
Cannot stop her head from turning back and
Forth as her mouth chews on air; and the man
Behind her snorts like a pig, wearing piss-
stained trousers and an ill-fitting wig.
Who are they? What are they? Where are they from?
There's one in a wheelchair, several on
Crutches, others crawling behind; how much
Is clear? They stare, do you see? They stare. These

Creatures, they're not just flophouse mystics,
Sidewalk savants, hash-puffing gurus in
Psycholinguistics, microstatistics,
Apocalyptic logistics—jostling
For attention amidst the rapidly
Sliding planes of unreality. Look
Again. You see? I think you do. They remind
You of you because they *are* you, because
They are *you*—the tainted, mangled waste-seed
Of that feinted, tangled misdeed, that barely
Stifled pressure-feed that cannot be
Disowned, postponed, condoned. They're beckoning;
Deny them no longer. There must be a
Reckoning for which the time is threatening.
Afflicted, restricted, evicted and
Constricted, they emerge from the limbo
Of the lost. Who is this young girl? You –
Her begetter – imagined her into
This half-life, you, her sole progenitor,
Propelled her into this shadow-realm, hurled
Her into this Overwhelm, knowing
Only terror at the heart of this
Under-realm, in which she is beset, by
Terror she is met, with ghosts. Hear them scream!
          Who is this woman now striding toward you?
Her names are Conception, Deception,
Election. Her name is Redemption.
Her hand extends – grasp it, enclasp it, and now
Disrobe. She yearns for you, returns for you,
Burns for your touch. Let her embrace you,
Let her be your judge, she wants to encase
You, to efface all those ghosts. Feel the warmth
Of her flesh? She burns for you. Sink into it,
Surrender, give into it, be tender;
She tells you her name: 'Deliverance and
Pleasure and Regeneration, Recon-
ciliation of Self.' See those gleaming lips;
Her words start to win you; her love could eclipse
What you've done. She steps before you: 'My name
Is Absolution – Absolution
Transfusion; behold me, the angel of
Mercy.' She raises her arms, emanating
Light, 'My name is Forgiveness. You're tired, you
Want to give in. Touch me', she says, 'Touch me
Now.' Her hand extends; he looks at her. 'No.'

She's gone. And in those after-moments, as
Daylight filters into the room, he feels
The bustling, deafening weight of all that he
Has done come flooding back to view.

'The weird real'

Michael Edwards, *At the Brasserie Lipp* (Carcanet) £9.99

THOMAS DAY

Paris coffee and croissants is the weird
real this morning, and a writing hand.
– Michael Edwards, *At the Brasserie Lipp*

'WEIRD' IS A WORD I remember hearing, and being struck by, while studying under Michael Edwards. It carried a certain weight: moments in Baudelaire, in Eliot, in Hill, were 'weird'. It felt like an acknowledgement that poetry, at its most potent, can disarm critical response. The weirdness was sometimes a source of fascination, sometimes an impediment to empathy, as if Edwards were pondering what made poet X unique, idiosyncratic, and, implicitly, quite unlike himself. Above all, the word bespoke a kind of penetrating perplexity that has its connection to another Edwardsian keyword, wonder.

'[T]he real' is 'weird', in section 28 of *At the Brasserie Lipp*, in that it is cause of wonder, but also because the otherness of the real resists the writer's attempts to render it in language, through language: so much so that the breakthroughs, when they come, seem mysterious, quasi-miraculous even. The poet, in Edwards's conception, aims to release the real by bringing to it a freshness of perception and a quality of wakeful attention, which draw the reader closer to the phenomena he has his sights on, or his ears or nose open to. By the same token, the felt presence of the phenomenal world is what the writing hand, working with imperfect material, grasps clumsily and belatedly at, hence 'and a writing hand' registering as a lumpen appendage in this opening sentence of this section – though it may be that we come closer to the real for the fact that the writing reflects this experience too. Releasing the real seems even harder here because the freshness has to be rescued from the dulling effects of cliché: how are we meant to wake up and smell the coffee when the evocations of Parisian life seem all too familiar: coffee, croissants, poets scribbling in literary cafés? Really? Yet note how these things are cunningly unsettled: '*Paris* coffee and croissants' is a shade different from 'Parisian', the noun employed as an adjective subtly suggesting that we are sampling the real thing rather than an imitation. And weird indeed that the plural nouns, 'coffee and croissants', should take a singular verb, 'is'. Is this conflation a means of distilling the delicate interplay of brasserie aromas, or does it introduce linguistic slippage, the hint of translationese, here, the sign of one no longer quite at home in the mother tongue, which is half-disclaimed, a few sections earlier, as 'my mother's tongue' (*At the Brasserie Lipp*, p. 54)? The former reading affirms the poem's fidelity to its real referents, even as the latter makes the speaker feel more real, more human in his lingual fallibility. The line break does its work too, emulating the way the attentive poet has to wait, listening intently to the silence the resistant world

initially puts up, until, as Edwards has explained, 'his language and the desired real collaborate [...] as he gives words to the world, the world gives him words'. It's the way the world gives him words that I think Edwards finds really weird.

These lines from Pope's *An Essay on Criticism* have apprised his understanding of poetry's capacity to apprehend the real:

> But true *Expression*, like th'unchanging Sun,
> *Clears*, and *improves* whate'er it shines upon,
> It *gilds* all Objects, but it *alters* none. (ll. 315–17)

But 'it *alters* none' and 'unchanging' are not quite Edwards's emphases. Poetry does alter in the sense that it imaginatively recreates whatever it shines upon, changing the way we see it in doing so: more than that, it opens out a world in the process of continual change, presenting things not only as they are, but as they might become – poetry points to possibility, to remember the title of one of Edwards's works of literary criticism.[1] *At the Brasserie Lipp* variously riffs on this idea:

> Poetry is a foreign language, way
> down inside one, guilty as hell
> like everything else, yet cannily innocent,
> in league with things to say them as they are
> or as they become in the resounding light.
> (*At the Brasserie Lipp*, p. 22)

These lines do improve upon, by way of gently qualifying, Pope's. While for Pope language is like the clarifying light, for Edwards the language of poetry emerges from murky depths analogous to hell's own. Poetry's murkiness is further implicit in its secondary likeness to 'everything else', which predicates a flattening of distinctions hardly conducive to flinging out broad the name of things in themselves, in all their uniqueness (Duns Scotus and haecceity crop up in a later section). Nor is it exactly clear how the poet's language collaborates with the desired real; 'in league with' casts this collaboration in a slightly insidious light, as befits its guilty state. Poetic expression, we might think, is not the light; indeed, the one thing differentiated from the amorphous mass of things in league with poetry is 'the resounding light', *ergo* the light must be other to poetry. Yet, one

---

1 Michael Edwards, 'Believing in Poetry', in *Literature and Theology* 25.1 (2011), pp. 10–19 (p. 11).

suddenly realises, that's not quite true, since the other thing singled out here is poetry. By some Escher-like logic which puts me in mind of the strange relationship between the I, the you, the third, and the who on the *other* side of you in 'What the Thunder Said', poetry aligns with that which is other to it, and by implication, with the otherness of the world at large. Poetry is – or rather it becomes – the light, a light which has the power to transform things, including poetry itself.

Another variation on this theme comes in the third poem of section 17:

> The light of childhood is clean, it adds
> like the sun nothing but itself to the scene
> in a café, maybe, a station, a sick-room.
> *Aux yeux du souvenir que le monde est immense*:
> wavering green creatures, plants without names,
> frogspawn, sticklebacks, the high wall, a whole
> ghostly reality, immortal fact.
> (*At the Brasserie Lipp*, p. 42)

The first two lines of this passage amplify the allusion to Pope's take on language and light in *An Essay in Criticism*, in part because of the way they ghost the heroic couplet. Spoken aloud, the caesura of the first line takes precedence over the line break, allowing 'clean' and 'scene' to chime the more emphatically, albeit an emphasis which the speaking voice, eliding the second line break, immediately takes the edge off of, as if to suggest that the light occasionally plays tricks. Listening to these lines also seems important because they turn on a pun: 'scene', as in a theatre, or a café, doubles as 'seen' as in 'visible' – a visible realised through the aural. The reciprocal role of sound in the resounding light of poetry is vital to its purchase on the real: poetry is in league with things to *say* them as they are', with the implication that saying them aloud – giving them corporeal form, by engaging the mouth, tongue and larynx – puts words and things in closer touch. '[T]o say [things] as they are' is another way of saying 'naming' them. 'a café, maybe, a station, a sick-room' are like surreal scene shifts flickering across the mind's eye as the light of childhood struggles to break through the fog of forgetting, but we might also hear this as someone wondering how best to name this newly created, or recreated, imaginative world. Adam's naming of the animals in the newly created world of Genesis is surely in play here, and with it the notion that Adamic language possessed the capacity to perfectly match signifiers to signifieds, thus to express the true essence of things in a way that later human languages could not. Bathed in 'the light of childhood', this certainly resembles a kind of prelapsarian first world, though it may be that the last of the suggested scene changes, 'a sick-room', is the most apt for a world on the cusp of the Fall. 'wavering green creatures, plants without names, / frogspawn, sticklebacks' transport us to a garden, wherein the naming of natural creation goes hand in hand with childlike wonder; 'the high wall' imparts a sense of sanctuary which imbues 'a whole' with an exultation comparable to Wordsworth's evocation of the vale of Grasmere as a kind of Eden in the final section of *The Recluse*: a place 'Made for itself; happy in itself, / Perfect Contentment, Unity

entire' (ll. 150-51). As with the near-couplet, the line break shatters the momentary illusion of self-contained perfection, since 'a whole' turns out to be just a part of a longer phrase. But the lack of completion attests a fallen world vibrant with possibility rather than one scarred by loss. 'frogspawn' looks forward to metamorphosis, and the 'wavering green creatures' and the plants that the archetypal gardener didn't get round to naming remind one that there is work still to be done, things to be learned. Possibility, not prevarication, is the force of the deceptively casual word 'maybe' which conditions the act of naming; or rather, prevarication, '*wavering* green creatures', is precisely what is transfigured.

The inversion of Baudelaire's line about the world appearing little to the eyes of memory speaks to this discourse of the real and the wondrous possible, but it is another French poet named in the first section of *At the Brasserie Lipp* who may have more to say to Edwards on these matters: Pierre Emmanuel. Emmanuel's early essay 'The Poet and Myth' makes the striking claim that, as Edwards summarizes it, 'the poet – that is, the person who handles words with the greatest knowledge and intimacy – is 'the stranger to names'.[2] This estrangement arises because the poet sees the world through the eyes of the child becoming aware of it, and naming it, for the first time; to the adult, the bond between word and thing has hardened through habitual association so that 'the name attached to it does not create it, but defines it' (ibid.). One might have thought that Edwards's argument about the language of poetry being in league with things to say them as they are presupposed their fundamental affinity, but if he follows Emmanuel on this, as I think he does, this is not the case; on the contrary, the poet's strangeness to names predicates a much looser link between words and the things they stand for. This would be another reason why the plants seen in the clean light of childhood in section 17 remain nameless; the sticklebacks are named as such, but our attention is drawn to the word's strange distance from the fish: it registers as a language experiment, someone trying out the word to see if it fits, but doing so as much for the sheer pleasure of the consonantal noise it makes, and for the pleasure of making it. This tendency of the child/nascent poet to experience language as a phonetic surface unfastened from meaning is explicitly at the fore of section 14:

> Listen to *bungalow*, wide-eared seven-year-old,
> in the small front room contained in your small
> measureless mind. And *verandah*, voiced
> by an unsolved aunt, prickly with secret
> and unseizable words. A queer
> *cupple* apparently living in a low
> bunga will tease your brain, until
> a softly whirring verandah flying past
> covers the sky in colours and waving giants.
> *Gardenshed* is no less magic – listen!
> *cupboard, doorway, passage*, all
> vibrating with what they name, speaking

2 Michael Edwards, 'Pierre Emmanuel', *Of Making Many Books: Essays on the Endlessness of Writing* (Basingstoke: MacMillan, 1990), pp 83–92 (p. 83).

from the strange warm beings to which they lead.
(*At the Brasserie Lipp*, p. 35)

Emmanuel on the strangeness of names might seem to have something in common with Saussure on the arbitrary nature of the sign, but Edwards, in his essay on Emmanuel, draws a crucial distinction. For Saussure, 'The word "tree" opens only to the idea *tree*, while the tree itself, left out of account and obliged to put down its roots in a dry and purely hypothetical reality, remains forever inaccessible' (p. 84), while for Emmanuel the gulf between words and things is a source of sorrow, and a symptom of man's exile from Eden, albeit a distressing distance which language can magically bridge:

> Without denying the distance between language and world, [Emmanuel] sees naming as an *act* (whereas for Saussure, with his view of language as an already existing structure, the mind seems to register names passively), and above all he understands the function of this act as conferring on a thing a new kind of being [...] giv[ing] it being 'in mind'. (ibid.)

Edwards, too, does not deny the distance between language and world:

> What do they know, these amiable aliens,
> that they speak their minds, they pluck their words
> from the world's tree regardless of Saussure,
> and hear them glittering among the spoons, the glasses?
> (*At the Brasserie Lipp*, p. 21)

Saussure is not refuted, but simply circumvented, and 'these amiable aliens', strangers to names (the line immediately preceding this passage also connects their alienation to 'the strangeness of adults'), speak their minds, not because they are opinionated, but in the sense that their speaking confers on things being in mind. Thus their words acquire physical presence, able to evoke the metallic tinkling of the spoons, the clinking of the glasses. The distance between language and the world does not altogether disappear, though, since what they and we 'hear' is a visual verb, 'glittering'. We are aware of the arbitrariness of language here, and yet 'glittering' has a sonic quality which could conjure up the subtle clatter of cutlery and crystalware; if words were being coined anew, 'glittering' might do just as well as 'clinking' or 'tinkling' (or '*brlnk*', the nonce word applied to the sound of a door swinging to in the first line of this section). And that's the point: words are being used by the poet as if for the first time, and ill-fitting as it is – or rather because it is ill-fitting – 'glittering' becomes one of those words which creates rather than merely defines or describes. And through this becoming the *real* meaning of the word is mysteriously born again: in conferring on things 'a new kind of being' they acquire the sheen of the newly minted, 'glittering'. The glittering is also the sprinkling of magic dust with which language transforms reality, the very magic that we're asked to listen to in '*Gardenshed*' in the previously quoted passage. There too Edwards has no truck with the Saussurian view of language as an already existing structure whereby the mind registers names passively; those italicised words that 'vibrat[e] with what they name' is a distinctly active process, rather like a

chemical reaction. To take the analogy one step further, language alters reality in the same way that heat (or light) acts on matter, exciting a kinetic energy that causes particles to vibrate, and then, as they cool, settle into a new arrangement. Perhaps the italics given to '*Gardenshed*', '*bungalow*' '*verandah*' and the other words visually record the effect of these vibrations that invite us to look at the world aslant, and it's notable that the particles, or characters, which make up '*Gardenshed*' have been reconstituted as one word, just as '*bungalow*' gets separated out, in the child / poet's mind, into two. The reality altered by language is not a dry and purely hypothetical reality as Saussure's is, but a 'strange' and 'warm' one, which is to say sensuously alive and active – might the warmth attest residual kinetic energy? – yet other. 'Our habitation is neither the real as it is, nor the poem, but the virtual reality glimpsed in poetry', Edwards writes in the essay on Emmanuel (p. 89), or as he puts it in the poem, 'a whole / ghostly reality'.

The role of memory, in this autobiographical poem, in transforming reality as it is, or as it was, needs pondering. 'The act / of memory changes', the final section of the poem tells us:

> Memory like
> photography is not realist art,
> today's light plays on each recovered scene
> as sunlight each day on each day's various faces.
> (*At the Brasserie Lipp*, p. 69)

Memory's infusion of the present moment, 'today's light', modifies the past; memory is an 'art' in that it is creative as well as recreative, and though photography is the art form it is explicitly compared to, the diction also claims non-realist kinship with the dramatic arts, '*plays* on each recovered *scene*'; 'various faces' supplies a hint of the personae and other dramatic procedures of much modernist poetry, and this leads into some lines which link memory to the multiplicity of the self:

> Memory is the name
> for the unknown occasional country where among
> the looming half-foreign me's the signs
> of the real and waiting other-me fitfully glint,
> the garden lilac, a Kingston street,
> appear sometimes, numinous, new-worldy.
> (*At the Brasserie Lipp*, p. 70)

The use of memory in poetry, and the attendant recovery and renewal of the real, effect another change, the change undergone by the self through the act of writing. If things *become* themselves through true expression, then so does the self; there is an otherness within the self, as there is in the real, which flickers into being in the poetic process: a potential other self or selves, the 'waiting other-me', the discovery of which is part of poetry's surprise and pleasure. Shakespearean metamorphosis is the model for this change in another section that revisits the poet's youth in Kingston-upon-Thames, where 'Memory cannot help / this ageing Bottom catch sight of that smell', the smell being the 'Indecently real' reek of a tannery (*At the Brasserie Lipp*, pp. 30-31). '*this* ageing Bottom' allows for a certain astonishment at the transformation of the self, which speaks to Edwards's sense of the unknown country into which writing, and ageing, lead you. But the 'this' also denotes a self-deprecating distance from this comic alter-ego which, comically, makes Bottom sound a little whiffy (like the tannery), as if an unpleasant discovery has been made. The 'I' who speaks, who exists in the present moment of writing, is not quite at one with the self-as-other in the poem, despite the illusion of presence created by that 'this'; Edwards's ageing Bottom is more like one of the self-parodic 'looming half-foreign me's' than the real 'waiting other-me', and in thinking of its foreignness we might recall the terms of Quince's astonishment at the metamorphosis: 'Bless thee, Bottom, bless thee. Thou art translated'.

Beckett's Krapp supplies another allusive model for memory and the multiple selves it engenders: section 9 takes us 'Down spools of time', and one cannot help but hear Krapp's *relish* of the word 'Spooool!' as he sorts through his autobiographical tapes, like a child toying with a weird word he has just discovered (cf. *'verandah'*). Edwards's book on Beckett, *Beckett, ou, le don des langues*,[3] which explores Beckett's decision to switch from English to French and back, might also have a bearing on the half-foreign metamorphic me's we encounter in this poem, since a similar decision has been crucial to Edwards's career and clearly underpins his poetics of the real. Reality is roused and encountered afresh when one names it in a foreign language, and when you adopt another tongue you become aware of another you: 'to speak a foreign language is to sense the real possibility of the self and the world changing'.[4] That, after years of living in France and writing in French, Edwards should

have returned to English for this latest collection, might be because English has begun to feel ever-so-slightly foreign, offering the poet the strangeness to names which he seeks, even needs. The poem wryly pre-empts this line of inquiry: 'Are you an English poet, they ask, or a French?' Pre-empts it, and promptly deflects it:

> I'm a Russian poet. I always write
> in a language I do not know. Myself,
> come to think of it, and I
> think of it often, am or is
> somewhat of a foreigner, alien to all
> I'd hoped to be.
> (*At the Brasserie Lipp*, p. 45)

The language he does not know, of course, is also the word made strange by its positioning at the end of that line, 'Myself', and the wavering over the form of 'to be' two lines later, which may be an awkward Englishing of Rimbaud's 'Je est un autre', further invites us to reflect on the self as other. And the speaker is right to correct himself here, since the present moment of writing which conditions 'I am' is superseded by the possibility of the self and the world changing, by the real and waiting other-me, for whom, we discover at the end of the book, we remain in waiting. There, the fiction of the present moment of writing, that all this has been composed while sitting at a café table, finally falls away, though it keeps alive the possibility that it could become a reality:

> What more can one say? I shall stroll the Seine,
> browse the bookshops, and maybe visit,
> one day soon, the Brasserie Lipp.

---

3 *Beckett, ou, le don des langues* (Montpellier: Editions Espaces, 34, 1998).

4 Michael Edwards, 'A Magic, Unquiet Body', in *Christianity and Literature*. 65.2 (2016), pp. 195–206 (p. 202).

From the Archive

Issue 151, May–June 2003

ROBERT MINHINNICK

Fellow contributors to this issue include David Kinloch, Edwin Morgan, Alison Brackenbury, Marilyn Hacker and Neil Powell.

THE FAIRGROUND SCHOLAR

So dream a little. The caff's art deco;
and outside it's Trieste not Trecco.
The arm of the Atlantic round your waist.

Though you seem to be a terrible flirt
there's no reason why you should get hurt:
the arm of the Atlantic round your waist.

Here's George W. Bush, come up from the ranch.
He'd like to beat us to death with an olive branch.
The arm of the Atlantic round his waist. [...]

Keeper of the Fire

JOHN FULLER

In memory of Saul Touster (1925—2018)

1

Among the googols of irrelevant facts today
Is the one I feared to find: a terminal date
To your career of distinction as poet and lawyer.

It is not only a shocking rent
In your personal fabric of space and time
But now a plain event in the public account

Occurring after the latest, and now the last
Of your fond communiqués of bravado,
Written 'from the edge of eternity.'

We had long exchanged these messages of affection
And wry good cheer, as though we had somehow given birth
To our own elderly selves, almost by accident.

Surprised at survival, dismayed at the vagaries
Of that weak organ of circulation and delay
Which turns hope or dismay into imperfect prayers.

2

We met in Buffalo in 1962, an ivy-creepered campus
With a famed collection of manuscripts,
A temple in wild country.

And you, the young Saul, gentle doyen
Of its welcoming Jewry, with your caressing speech
And your Harold Lloyd glasses, proclaiming

Rosenzweig's idea of the virtues of Judaism
As a fire in a clearing in a wilderness,
Shedding its light, but rooted to the spot.

Christians take torches from this fire,
Dashing into the darkness to bring its light
To the rest of the forest. But the light of these torches

Would expire unless relighted at the source.
This was your idea of a university:
Keeper of the fire, for torches to be rekindled there.

But I was no Christian, and I then knew nothing
Of my eighth share of your brethren's blood,
An ignorant child of a monstrous decade.

You were reasonably to cite Sheinson's Haggadah:
'How is it possible to speak of or to God in 1946?'
Having to deal with the monsters we ourselves had created.

Here, then, at the cradle of the hopeful 1960s,
The DP camps barely five years closed
And poems proclaiming at best the smallest decencies

While in the country of the Vile Antagonist
Your Catholic President was to declare himself,
As if already extinguished, a kind of donut.

And the young prepared simply to enjoy themselves
For ever and ever, as though that would dispel those
shadows
Etched into evil, that could be printed off again.

3

A snow-belt winter saw head-high ploughfuls
Packed where once we parked our battered De Soto,
The cistern freezing in our grey-and-green apartment

Where Prue cheered us with Gogol-Mogol
(Egg yolk and Demerara) while I marked papers
On the intentions of Nashe's *Unfortunate Traveller*

And Sophie practised walking, making her first friend
With Polish Penny next door. We pulled her,
Rosy in her snow-suit and sled, through the approach

To Niagara where the ice stood a foot thick
On the spray side of the coppice of trees,
And they said we were crazy to take her out.

And our season of introductions was well advanced:
Turkey and apple pie with Mrs Abbott
And her ugly bull-dog, unnervingly called Sophia.

Party after party, housewarmings and readings,
You, Saul, as the prime chairman of good cheer
Along with Aaron, and Al, and the commanding Oscar.

Provider of punch and appeaser of the Pos,
Sculptor of verses of the still life,
Frozen moments aching for perfection.

You worked in a vein of passionate directness
In the admired manner of Americans (the latest was Lowell)
Whose lives were always alive, still but not dead

Leading the past to its perfection and regrets,
Like an apple and its amorous adventures,
Like an apple that might as well be a person.

You were yearning for the happiness that poetry
Tells us we may work to deserve
If we can understand the warnings within it.

Your Salo was a creation of the night,
Vagrant and dispossessed, with a grudge against time
And a nose for the winds and restlessness of the city.

4
Spring melted in Allegany
Where we all took to the woods
In a green-boarded cabin dripping from its eaves

And the woodchucks and chipmunks
Scuttling in the brush
Muttered their farewells to winter.

Idle days of young families together,
Free of their students and the dark city,
A controlled experiment in creative living.

Tasha scribbling, Sophie testing
Her toes, and madcap Jonnie
Shy behind Helen's dirndl.

Prue managing the imperfect plumbing
With recourse to the stream below
For the dunking of dishes.

I quoted our favourite sage's
'And now she cleans her teeth into the lake'
As an unusual communion with nature

And it pleased your calculating mind
As another kind of legal fiction
To our rights *usque ad inferos.*

Parents in damp ponchos, vying
In badminton and *bouts rimés*,
Upright as bears in holiday attire

With steak on an open fire and yams
In the embers which you tendered
With recitations and a hopeful stick.

And as we performed these pleasures,
There darted between the trees
The orange eyes of racoons.

5
Our year was soon gone, across
The continent and back to New York.
You took our trunks to Railway Express

And saw us off at the downtown docks
Where the ocean waited (who names the seas
Since no one lives on them?).

You lamented the passing of time
As what it can come to seem:
The lapse of affection in divergence.

And in all the following decades
What became of the feel and length of our lives
Which now appeared as descriptions and rumours?

Your marriages expired, like unrenewed
Permits for happiness. Your letters
Were sometimes thick with poems.

There was gossip from the poetic front:
Olsen the Queen Bee; the Pos, now married,
Beating up the twice-beat Corso.

Your parties went swimmingly,
'And those who couldn't swim
Just floated off.' And there was good advice:

'Clear away the debris ... let your voice
Come upon you like an Indian from ambush,
At a casual turn in the path.'

Later, Brandeis and administration
Claimed your pacifying talents.
You worked on the great Holmes and the Civil War

And at Lowell's funeral were reminded not only of Shaw
And his Black regiment, but of poets
As unexceptional, their deaths as men.

You also met Irene in 1977, woman
'With Irenic qualities,' yours
For more than forty years.

6
For whom, now, these words are intended,
Though anyone may read them, since
The private also has its public occasions.

Dear Saul, we should have seen more of you.
That time you were in London
And called, but we were in Wales!

In your eighties you leaped an Oxford gate
And pretended not to be bothered
By torn trousers: an English reaction.

You lamented with us the renewal of the monstrous,
The forgetting that is the prelude to ignorance,
The march on reason, the release of hatred.

And you wrote your own late poems of remembrance,
Reminding us that the stories we tell are the real truth
And that even judges should undertake a study of poetry.

And when we met you at that Dream Hotel
In the underwater blues of its mirrored lobby
You were still that enthusiast of life we had long known

And you expounded in the Met on Morandi
And his luminous *natura morta* with a gravity
That came of knowing how our lives

Are never still, but surely end up in stillness
And the fire that is the fire of knowledge
Is also the fire that will one day consume us.

From the Nahuatl

HUGH THOMSON

1: Ahuízotl: The Dog of Water

I am hairless. I am the dog
that eats the bodies after slaughter.

I am the dog
that waits beneath the water.

At the end of my tail
I have a human hand.

I give no quarter.
I am the dog

who lives beneath the water.
You will not hear me bark.

You will feel my bite.
I will take you in the night.

I am the dog
that waits beneath the water.

2: Tlaltecatzin's Song to his Mistress

You've undressed in front of the princes
and are lying, invitingly,
on a pillow bed of blue and yellow feathers,
your eyes like toasted maize,

knowing full well you will be left
abandoned, and you will leave yourself
with the flesh stripped
from you bare, *ximaaz.*

I still want you.
My heart knows it –
my heart is overflowing –
my heart knows the truth.

3: Xipe Totec: The God of Spring

My skin is flayed
and laid back on me:
a fine brocade
of knots and veins.

It stings, like antiseptic
on a cut. I am the king
of self-inflicted pain. I am
the re-emergent, caustic Spring.

Moctezuma

My house has many chambers.
In some they will serve you chocolate.
In others I have the quetzal bird, and snakes.

They have seen men riding on deer –
I killed the man who told me so –
and a bird with mirrored eyes,
a monster with two heads.

I look in the obsidian mirror
and see myself dark and lost
and receding to some other chamber
whose name I do not know.

A Glyph for the Common Man

*'King Jaguar Paw celebrated the completion of the
17th katun, and let his own blood from his tongue.'*
Stone Stela 39, Tikal, 376 AD

And how would a glyph
to the common man read?

To the thousands who built Uxmal,
Chichén Itza, Palenque, Cobá;
who raised the stelae at Copán
or the pyramids of grand Calukmal,
commemorating Great Jaguar Paw,
six feet tall Pacal,
and Lord Water of Caracol,
axe murderer of Double Bird?

*'I died young, poor, malnourished
and miserable, so that a few
could be remembered in stone.'*

'A Calculated Act of Goddess': on Robert Graves

GREVEL LINDOP

THE POET AND MYTHOGRAPHER Robert Graves was a great teller of tall stories; and most of the stories he told were true. There was the one, for example, about being left for dead after the Battle of the Somme in 1916: his parents received the dreaded telegram telling them he had died of wounds; after his recovery he was able to read the announcement of his own death in the *Times*.

Then there was the one about being bitten by a viper in the Pyrenees – the Pyrenean viper being, according to Graves, 'eight times more lethal than the English'. 'After the first pain and vomiting,' he recalled, 'my eyesight began to fail. A small silver spot appeared in the centre of my field of vision, which gradually enlarged into an island with sharply defined bastions; the shores spread wider and wider, as though I were nearing it across a sea. When I started to walk home, I could not see where I was going; and then the island began slowly to revolve in a clockwise direction.'[1]

He recognised his vision as the 'Silver Island' or 'Revolving Island' to which the sacred king in a range of ancient cultures (Celtic, Greek, Egyptian...) was said to go after his sacrificial death. It is, Graves claimed, 'seen prophetically by him when his heel is bitten by the serpent or scorpion, or pricked with the (presumably) poisoned arrow.' Again he survived, to undergo another visionary experience – this time pharmacological – when, in 1960, he took mescaline with the mushroom expert R. Gordon Wasson, and experienced visions of sailing through the green marble colonnades of an underwater temple complete with 'massive sunken statuary', and 'lovely, live, naked caryatids'. He felt 'capable of solving any problem in the world... But the sensation of wisdom sufficed – why should I trouble to exploit it?'[2]

But the strangest of Robert Graves's stories concerned the fates of the three publishers to whom he submitted *The White Goddess*. Biographers have recorded the story; none has investigated it. But it deserves scrutiny. Graves told it at the end of a 1957 lecture at New York's YWHA – now the '92nd Street Y'. After summarizing the book's arguments, and telling how it came to be written, Graves continued:

> I offered *The White Goddess* in turn to the only publishers I knew who claimed to be personally concerned with poetry and mythology.
>
> The first regretted that he could not recommend this unusual book to his partners, because of the expense. He died of heart failure within the month.
>
> The second wrote very discourteously, to the effect that he

could not make either head or tail of the book, and could not believe it would interest anyone. He died too, soon afterwards.

But the third, who was T.S. Eliot, wrote that it must be published at all costs. So he did publish it, and not only got his money back, but pretty soon was rewarded with the Order of Merit, the Nobel Prize for Literature, and a smash hit on Broadway.

Very well, call these coincidences. But I beg you not to laugh yet! Wait! I beg you not to laugh, unless you can explain just why the second publisher should have dressed himself up in a woman's panties and bra one afternoon, and hanged himself from a tree in his garden. (Unfortunately, the brief report in *Time* did not specify the sort of tree.)

Was that a blind act of God, or was it a calculated act of Goddess? I leave the answer to you; all I know is that it seemed to me natural enough in its horrid way.[3]

The notion that Graves submitted his book to just three publishers is easily dismissed. The first draft of his massive and unorthodox treatise on myth and poetic inspiration, proclaiming the need for poets (and European civilisation as a whole) to return to the worship of an inspiring Goddess, was written in the course of a few weeks during 1942. His agent A.P. Watt immediately offered it to several publishers, amongst them Cape, Cassell and J.M. Dent, none of whom figures in our story. It was eventually taken, in an enlarged version, by a small New York publisher, Creative Age, and in London by Faber and Faber, where T.S. Eliot himself made the decision, and – evidently with a good deal of relish – wrote the blurb ('This is a prodigious, monstrous, stupefying, indescribable book'). The 'smash hit' which Graves's Goddess bestowed on Eliot was *The Cocktail Party*, a surprise Broadway success in 1950. Eliot received his Novel Prize in November 1948, six months after the book's publication.

But what about the two publishers who turned the book down? Did they, as Graves claimed, pay for their editorial judgment with their lives? It was known that Graves's agent A.P. Watt had submitted the book to Charles Williams, a poet who was also a senior editor at Oxford University Press, and who died suddenly in 1945. Had he personally rejected the book? It was at this point that my own investigations began. The immense files of Graves's correspondence (now at St John's College, Oxford) were, when I first took up the question, still located in the house at Deía, Mallorca, where Graves had lived until his death in 1985. I was told that there were no letters from Williams in the files. To make sure, however, I enquired whether there were any letters at all from Oxford University Press. Indeed there were; and one of them was signed with the merest blue ripple of a pen, unintelligible unless one happened to be familiar with the

---

1 Robert Graves, *The White Goddess* (Manchester: Carcanet Press, 1997), pp. 295–6.

2 'The Poet's Paradise', *Oxford Addresses on Poetry* (London: Cassell, 1962), pp. 123–4.

3 Appendix B, *The White Goddess* (Manchester: Carcanet Press, 1997), p. 504.

scrawled 'CW' that was Williams's usual signature:

> My Dear Robert Graves, [it ran] I had better say at once that I have failed. I am very sorry indeed, not that it will make any difference to you, because you will get the book published easily enough, but because I should very much have liked the Press to publish it.... It seemed to me a thrilling description of the way the poetic mind works, and very valuable on that account....I have said all this here, and pressed it as far as I can....It is, of course, impossible for me to write like this and not to feel something of a fool when I know the MS. is going back to Watt. But there I must rely on your generosity.

Williams enclosed a pompous letter from Sir Humphrey Milford, head of the Press, regretting that O.U.P. could not publish Graves's 'study of the poetic mind' but must give priority to 'specialist works: the remaining volumes of the Oxford History [of England], the History of English Literature, and so on.' Williams died suddenly of an intestinal complaint ten months later (not, one notes, 'of heart failure within the month'). Clearly he had wanted to publish *The White Goddess*. Equally clearly, he was one of the victims Graves had in mind. But what about the other, who had died in such bizarre circumstances?

Graves had mentioned 'the brief paragraph in *Time*'. I searched the contents and indexes of *Time* magazine in the 1940s and found nothing. It seemed possible, though, that '*Time*' had been a slip for 'the *Times*' – perhaps the *New York Times*: a natural error if, as seemed likely, the tale had been passed to Graves by his friend Tom Mathews, an editor at *Time* magazine. I had an obliging friend (it was Charles Rzepka of Boston University) check the *Times* index, and he struck gold:

PUBLISHING EXECUTIVE FOUND DEAD
Special to the New York Times.
Irvington on Hudson, N.Y., July 19 [1946]. Alexander J. Blanton, 45 years old, a vice president of Macmillan Company, publishers, was found this afternoon hanging from a tree behind his home on Riverview Road here. Dr Amos O. Squire, Westchester medical examiner, listed the death as a 'suicide while mentally disturbed.'

We had our man. (The Macmillan archive confirmed that the company had rejected *The White Goddess* on 16 April 1946.) Still, the matter of Blanton's attire on the fatal day remained unresolved, and it was hard to see how any public source could settle it, whatever New York's literary grapevine might have transmitted.

At this point help came from an unexpected quarter. I was corresponding with an American political historian, Raymond Polin, about something quite different. Polin mentioned that he admired Robert Graves, and I told him of my quest. 'That's easy,' said Polin. 'My son's an attorney. I'll ask him to make a Freedom of Information request and get the medical examiner's report.' It was hard to believe that things could be so simple; and I had become resigned to thinking the idea a mere pipedream, when a bulky package arrived from the US. Its contents exceeded anything I had imagined possible. Not only did it contain the death certificate and the medical examiner's report—they agreed on 'Asphyxiation by hanging while mentally disturbed' – but there were two quarto sheets of typescript, clipped together and headed 'VILLAGE OF IRVINGTON, N.Y. / POLICE DEPARTMENT'. It was the report of the investigating officer. Dated July 19, 1946, it read:

> At about 12.25 P.M. I received a call from Mr W.R. Clark of Riverview Road, Irvington stating that he was over at the Blanton residence putting mail in their house as they are away. He said he noticed the form of a woman hanging from a tree in their back yard. I notified Chief McCall of same.
>
> The Chief and I went to said residence and found, hanging by the neck from a tree about 25 feet from the house, one Alex Blanton, age 45 years. He was dressed in his wife's clothing consisting of the following: a small black hat, yellow sweater, green skirt, tan stockings, black pumps, earings [sic], silver bracelet, a girdle, lipstick, and a string of beads around his neck. He had placed a small strap that was doubled around his neck and pulled it tight. Then he took a large luggage strap about one inch wide with a slip buckle and placed it around his neck and over the limb of a tree. There was a table by the tree as if he stood on same and jumped off. Dr Smith was notified and responded immediately. Dr Smith, Chief McCall, and myself cut him down from the tree. Dr Squires was notified and had the body removed to the Edwards Funeral Parlor in Dobbs Ferry where he will view same. The Chief and I searched the house for a note but could find no trace of any. The house was not disrupted.
>
> We found his wallet on the dresser in his room with $47 in bills and 59 cents in change. On the sun porch was a bottle of whiskey, three quarters empty, and the door was opened as if he went out that way. Mrs Blanton and family left yesterday for the Rhode Island Shore for a vacation. Mr Blanton went to business yesterday, but none of the neighbours saw him come home last night. Mr Blanton was the Vice President of the McMillan Publishing Company of New York City. His firm was notified and a Miss Doris Pattee an executive said firm will notify Mrs Blanton.
>
> Dr Smith said death was caused by strangulation.
>
> Also found on the dresser was his watch and his pen knife. Chief McCall has the money and watch in the safe.
>
> Dr Squires gave his verdict as suicide.
>
> Officer E.J. Foley

So the story outlined by Graves was true. What was its meaning? Any connection with *The White Goddess* can safely be ruled out. So can auto-erotic strangulation: no one drinks three quarters of a bottle of whiskey and goes out into the garden for that. The clothing (the 'small black hat', the 'string of beads') seems oddly particular; did Blanton intend his suicide to convey some message to his wife, whose grim parody he must have appeared? Was his death the tragedy of a crossdresser or a transsexual unable to articulate his need except through this final extremity? It remains enigmatic. But for Graves, the story offered irresistible temptation as the climax of a tumultuously successful, crowd-pleasing lecture. Blanton's fate became part of the mystique of *The White Goddess*. Robert Graves didn't know or care much about Alexander Blanton. But there was a cruel side to his nature; and after all, he could never resist a good story.

Olympia and other poems

HEATHER TRESELER

Olympia

Manet aimed for the pantheon but became a pariah
with his portrait of a courtesan, her bright white
crinoline body unfurling like a flag of surrender,

her come-hither look as startling now as in 1863.
So too, the black servant giving her mistress
side-eye appraisal of this latest provocation,

no stranger to how a woman might manage
the fact that her imperiled body is for sale.
This is not love on auction. And you and I

are not in Paris, considering the original. Friends,
would-be lovers, a black man and a white woman,
we sit in a posh café three thousand miles from

the first blush of scandal, crowds so incensed
the Salon hired a pair of constables to stand guard
beside the bold prostitute and her bouquet-bearing

servant whom they hung over the doorway, beyond
the mob's reach or desecration. Overhead, the stark
line of her naked body must have looked like an altar

on which something of value – a fattened goat, a ruddy
boy, a coveted reputation – might be sacrificed in ritual
expiation. We think of burghers, men who enjoyed

their cigars and courtesans, the leisure of not having
to pretend to love someone, able to buy satisfaction
by the hour, outright. Of course Manet offended them.

We savour gin and tonics, our historical progress.
When we are out together, it is not a scandal. Not
in tidy liberal Concord where 'Black Lives Matter'

placards dot Yankee lawns with their daylilies
and dachshunds. Here, Thoreau refused to pay
his poll tax and spent all of one night in prison.

Here, in essays and speeches, Fuller and Emerson
tried to exhume buried rights of slaves and women,
claiming the necessity of emancipation, education,

enfranchisement as the civic *sine qua non*. We teach
at local colleges. We are for the left and possibly
for each other. We talk freely and flirtatiously

of the prostitute's pert breasts, each a delicate
mouthful; a proprietary hand she holds beneath
an oval navel; an orchid, tucked like a cattle tag,

behind her ear. We debate whether the terrified
glint in her eyes is part of the painting's seduction.
If wounding fear endures as a source of attraction,

which also seems wrong to admit or feel: how much
her frankness appeals, the theatre of all that desiring.
But it is the black servant, you posit, who bends

the shock of image to the arc of story. She shows
the viewer how to regard her mistress, pretending
to be the master of her fate and fees, feigning

indolence in a bare foot, slid from its heeled slipper.
The servant's gaze tells us we ought to know better,
we ought to see beyond this erotic tableaux vivant.

For who will buy the harlot's favors when her orchid
has gone rank, when azure skin is pocked with blistered
chancres? The servant holds flowers from some patron

still willing to obscure procurement with courtly flora,
a reliquary gesture. But no gallant will rescue her from
poverty, age, a venereal abscess gouging out a cheek

or nose, syphilitic delusion. Not even the church will
help her, or any of her urchins, then. She had better
have a cache of cheap gin, laudanum for the pain,

a shack in back country, a good store of grain,
a cord of thick rope or a tub with a drain. We raise
our half-emptied glasses to the doomed nude,

the worldly servant whose gaze spells out debacle,
and the painter who tracked his era's lengthening
shadow, putting us up for the bidding, up for sale.

After Catullus

Stoplights, school-buses dawdling by sports' fields,
  so many Subarus with becalmed dogs riding
shotgun. Traffic exists to test, they say, Christian
  patience for our fellow travelers. Or to teach
Zen detachment from the hurry of temporality.
  Or to remind atheists of all the other ways
we deliberately waste time. *Otium*, Romans called
  it, those builders and sons of empire wary of
leisure's slide into idleness. My hatchback hums,
  self-contenting machine, through the hectic
streets. I clutch and shift, foot to foot, on levers
  demanding pressure and touch. I long to be
home, naked, free from workday's clock, clothes,
  heels, politic notations. Do my neighbors,
stuck in this traffic, admiring their hair, phone,
  or relatively even teeth imagine the blue
film in my head where you take me again – *again* –
  in a high, low, or darkened bed, ravishing
my mouth, kneading my hungry breasts like bread?

Liturgy

This too is high mass:
my hurry of hands,
since I am overcome
with want and need
to have your warming
breath inside my body.

In the fourth gospel,
a god disguised as
language becomes flesh,
dwells among us.
Sentenced, we must
earn the predicate

of transitive release,
the proper noun of me
turned from symbolic
heft, from the music
my name makes in
your mouth to bread

of flesh, gently torn
in holy ravishing.
Suddenly, in the
middling, you leapt
from bed: fevered,
I'd let my dress fall

to the floor: you
pluck it from its
unboned heap,
smooth it across
a high-backed
chair. I trace your

curved collarbone
and think of how
prairie's horizon
was called once
'hemline of heaven'
as I kiss the bevel

in your clavicle's
key and feel your
chest's long door
turn open under
me: I step into the
house of your body

and greet a rogue
god hidden there
like the last word,
a transitive verb,
the fleshly god who
dwells between us.

Changes Made and other poems

BETSY ROSENBERG

Changes Made

No longer care to be a flying squirrel
stretched to the limit
eyes wide open,
gliding fiercely while I forage,
tickled by the draft
on my creamy underside.

I'm going to change my furry grey
for a gossamer white
float serene as dandelion fluff,
rely on drag to slow my descent
with love before I fade away,
there'll be some changes made today

there'll be some changes made.

Canal

I'm here
ready to enter the New Year
known also as the
Day of Remembrance
when 'Erie Canal' self-sings in my brain
with ancestors moving through it
from Buffalo to Cleveland
'Low bridge, everybody down
Low bridge for we're coming to a town'
and Daddy survives calamity
singing chin to chest
in his best bass-baritone
fifteen years on the Erie Canal
with an old mule named Sal
seven years since he
twelve since Jesse
thirteen since Jon
passed through the locks of a lifetime.

Mixed Blessings

Hashishin bard of the suq in his youth, he
would chalk little aphorisms on a slate:
Jolly potatoes ee-ai-o
Cubanelles for the very passionate
Apples of Eden red and green
Marrows that make dreams come true
Onions to keep your peepers clean
Sometimes a louche-looking rabbi
would loiter near him at the counter
and hand out blessings with
printed instructions
to sheepish customers like me.

Protean

This time I was a tuft of algae
holding fast,
a cuttlebone blanching on the sand.
I swear I could feel
the tedium
of tides, rust-stained mountains
mantle of the world
power of decay at the core,
and lying on my side
for a moment
I was part of creation,
the qualia of earthly life
striving with
the terrifying all.

Fastidious Fly and other poems

Nicola Healey

Fastidious Fly

A fly was drowning in my water glass.
I tipped it out and it clung onto a blade of grass
like a windsurfer.
　　　　　It steadied itself and then
meticulously cleaned its face, like a cat.

It lifted each iridescent wing
and smoothed them down with thread-thin legs,
closing them into place like a pair of shears,
glinting.
　　　　Then it took off.

I could have swallowed all that
intricate effort-to-be;
it wouldn't have tasted of anything.

A long-tailed tit

inching down a branch
of the willow tree
to reach a suet shell.

She doesn't mind that I'm
standing right there.
I am peripheral

in a good way.
I try to expel
my humanness

with a held breath.
Her eyes are dots
like poppy seeds.

I'm at rest.
Her small living matters
more than success.

Spirit Level

When you are ill, you are always working
on getting well. When you're well,
what you were aiming for seems only
air – the horizon is around you

not ahead. Spinning dancers
fix their gaze on a single
spot. But we must live with vert-
igo, and loss of balance. I used

to be hypnotised by
the bubble in a spirit level:
I'd watch my dad check if surfaces
were level or plumb as though he was

testing the lie of the world, and had
the power to make it settle. I felt
sorry for the forever trapped mini-
sphere; yet with its one perfect

purpose, it was an oracle.
Was it from this drop of air
I thought giving all to one
thing made a human useful?

escape and other poems

MINA GORJI

The Wasp

who makes no honey gave us ink.
In early spring oak galls appear:
darkening in autumn
they gestate.

Emerging into English light,
this tiny emigrant
was smuggled in Aleppo oak –
an alien acorn.

Charango

The Armadillo lives alone
in armour,
plates of dermal bone,
scale lapping scale
in compact rows –
protective carapace
prized for resonance.

escape,

/ɪˈskeɪp/
flee,
get free
like Daedalus
like Icarus.
Oute of youre lace
into the desert,
jump –
like electricity
escapes
when atmospheric pressure
is removed,
like leaves,
at the time of flowering,
escaping from their buds,
jump
or a spaceship
escaping from Earth
at 11.2 kilometres
a second
jump
elude,
escape
and lightly pass
the bitter pain
of purgatory,
the name of which
escapes me.

Beside the river

we look up:
so many shooting stars!
A flash, and then they
seem to slow:
one after another,
flash and fade.

These are not stars
but landing lights –
not blazing out,
but coming home.

TWO BROTHERS left Tblisi, Gorjistan, and travelled to the desert in Iran. No one knows why they left, or what they were escaping. They married two sisters and settled in Yazd. But their children moved out to the capital or followed trade routes to India.

My maternal grandparents in an army ship, leaving Madras for Liverpool, escaping the Djinn that took three of their children. They moved on to Edinburgh so grandfather could extend his training as a surgeon, FRCS. A few years later, 1947, Partition. They stayed in Britain.

Their own grandparents had left Iran for the wealth and seeming glamour of the British Empire – India, Hong-Kong, Singapore. They traded in opium and indigo, animal skins. Grandfather went to missionary school in Madras. They didn't use his real name, *Mohammad Taqui* – it sounded too foreign.

Grandmother was born in Singapore. Her teachers called her *Daisy*. Her name was *Shahtaj*. Tango was her favourite dance. Her grandfather, *M.A. Namazie*, had made a fortune in rubber. In 1930, he built one of the island's first cinemas, *The Capitol Theatre*. The *Straits Times* that year called it:

a thing of romance,
a dream solidified.

It screened the first-run English language films. Once a week grandmother was driven there to watch a matinee. On the domed ceiling of the Capitol, sculptures of winged horses, a mosaic of the twelve zodiac signs. Romance. The Great Depression – the price of rubber fell. Namazie died of a heart attack. Grandmother's years at medical school were cut short by marriage. She left Singapore for India in 1936, five years before the Japanese invasion.

1971. My mother, recently married, travelling by plane from London to Tehran – she didn't feel as though she was escaping. Eight years later, flying back to London, she did.

Tehran, 1979. Outside my window, mountains. The highest, *Damavand.* Visiting my uncle north of the city, I fell into a drift of snow, chin deep. At school, in the playground, I stepped in the warm wet tar. Just to feel it underfoot, to mark its perfect glossy blackness. It clung to my shoe. Soon we would be leaving.

We could see it changing from the window of our apartment. Demonstrations. Tanks. Soldiers. We could hear chanting. There were blackouts. Sitting in our flat, surrounded by boxes and crates packed with antique furniture – dark wood carved with tiny Chinese figures, men with long beards, ladies under cherry trees, curling clouds, dragons. It had travelled from Singapore to India, India to London and then to Iran, part of my grandmother's and then my mother's *trousseau.* The delivery men wouldn't take it – no antiques could leave the country. They were tightening the borders. People grew ingenious – hid gold coins in jars of jam, jewellery in the hollow of a carved-out heel. Our toys were given to the local hospital – I knew that we were leaving.

London, SW13, 1980. At five years old, I dreamed of firing squads. Flinched when I saw policemen. But there was warmth and family and love. Masala omelette, sweet with fried onions. Rice pudding, golden with saffron.

45 Lowther Road. I felt safe in that house, with its greengage trees, the secret musty smell of garden shed, the bright pink and purple swirls, paisley patterns on the duvet that crackled static when we huddled underneath. She'd whisper prayers until we fell asleep and blow them over us, to keep us safe.

Patterns. The antique Persian carpet in my grandparents' house
    stretched into the afternoons. I used to jump between
    the different coloured panels, making up stories, dreaming. Tiny feet, treading over rooftops of a miniature world:

Cyprus trees and citadels,
    palaces with copper domes,
        leopard chasing antelope,
    the moon in silver scimitar,
gardens full of roses.
    So many stories,
        knotted into silk.

Persepolis. One of my relations met Agatha Christie walking in the ruins of Persepolis. When I visited, it was almost empty. Winged bulls. A lizard darting over sand. *They say the lion and the lizard keep / The courts where Jamshýd gloried and drank deep.* Ruins of an empire. Perhaps if the Shah had not held that infamous party, none of this would have happened. Millions spent, monarchs, presidents, sultans, ambassadors, movie stars, all invited to Persepolis, to witness the greatness of the Persians. Decadence: 159 chefs, bakers, and waiters, all flown in from Paris. Roasted peacock, caviar, crystal, Limoges china. Thousands of snakes, scorpions and lizards, cleared from the site; zoologists took the

unknown species away, packed into special jars. Pine trees were planted in the desert. *Bekhab Cyrus, ma beed-areem.* Sleep on, Cyrus, we are awake.

Nightingales. Visiting Shiraz in 1932, Rabinderath Tagore wanted to hear the legendary *Bulbul of Shiraz*, but his trip fell at the wrong time of year. Anxious to please the famous poet, Mirza Ibrahim commissioned a mechanical bird to be made, containing a recording of the nightingale in full song. When you turned a handle, it would sing. Nightingale – symbol for poetry, lyric voice. *That ancient voice was heard at once by emperor and clown.* A voice to console the homesick. To soothe the heart of Ruth, standing in the alien corn. That Shiraz nightingale spoke to the Bengali poet in a language that was universal, at a time when the internationalist movement was in full swing. Tagore's great admirer Yeats described a mechanical nightingale in 'Sailing to Byzantium', *Of hammered gold and gold enamelling / To keep a drowsy Emperor awake; / Or set upon a golden bough to sing / To lords and ladies of Byzantium / Of what is past, or passing, or to come.*

Underneath an apple tree in Highgate, John Keats, inspired by a nightingale's song. In a wood on the edge of Helpston, a village on the brink of the Lincolnshire fens, John Clare, who shared a publisher with Keats, transcribed the nightingale's song in words. 1889, just over a decade after Clare's death, the first birdsong was recorded mechanically. Ludwig Koch, a precocious 8-year-old, made a recording on his father's phonograph. He was to arrive in England an exile from Nazi Germany in 1936. His recordings were acquired by the BBC and established the first natural history sound archive. Birdsong and exile. When you turn the handle, a nightingale still sings. A summer song, from long ago. A song of all that's passing.

Tehran, back again. Stranger to the place. Plane trees still lined the boulevards, water still ran down from the mountains in *joob* along the roadsides. In the park, a man was still selling balloons. You could still smell corn on the cob roasting on charcoal. The Japanese garden was still there, with its ornamental trees and rocks and raked gravel. But the park was renamed, *Laleh.* And the dress code had changed: you had to look as drab as possible, to avoid notice. No bright clothes. No make-up. I didn't mind wearing the *roosaree* (head-scarf). It was an adventure. I was in disguise.

Sitting in our old flat on Boulevard Keshavarz (formerly Boulevard Elizabeth) refusing to accept tea or sweets (*Quality Street)* from the tenants who had claimed it as their own. A modern, stylish flat. Earthquake proof. We had run away, they said. We were never coming back. *Don't eat the sweets,* my mother warned us. *Don't accept their hospitality. They are trying to take our flat.* Persephone.

Behind the metal gates of my great-aunt's house, you could wear what you wanted. We swam in the little pond and watched my grandmother shell broad beans, hollowing out watermelon skins for us to sail like boats on the little pond. The watermelons arrived in an open-top truck and were rolled down into the cellar. Every day she would take one and cut it for us and make juice from what was left. The garden had two tall dusty persimmon trees, the round orange fruit high out of reach. There was a pomegranate. The gardener said he'd cut off my nose if I picked one.

Inside was dark; a cool terrazzo floor. Sometimes, at night, we'd hear the scuttle of cockroaches – *soosk* – their sickly sweet smell. Upstairs, a room was always closed off. Rolled up carpets. Mothballs. Boxes full of books, left behind. I sat there in the half-light, reading, not *Lolita*, but a novel by de Sade. Bodies around a tree. How detached it seemed. How distant. Outside was fear.

Inside the contemporary art museum, a giant newspaper boat. Knives suspended from the ceiling.

Saddam was bombing Tehran. Mum told us the noise was thunder in the mountains. Then the windows shattered. Adults gathered around the radio. My great aunt refused to go into the cellar. If a bomb hit the house, she wanted to die straight away, not get trapped underground. Every night, sirens, bombs, anti-aircraft guns. Every morning, warm bread for breakfast, mint, feta cheese, hot tea. Sometimes crisp, cool *kharboozeh*, a pale green melon from Masshad. Very good with bread and cheese.

Noon o paneer o kharboozeh,
Bokhor bebeen che khoshmaze!

My dad would teach us the rhyme:

Bread and cheese and kharboozeh,
Eat and see how delicious!

It didn't work in translation.

Bombers were targeting the airport. As our plane took off, you could feel the relief, smell it: the adults all lit up.

Heathrow airport always smells the same: rubber, tarmac. We soon reached home. SW13. Its air of quiet moderation. Semi-detached houses with magnolia trees. Pancake races round the duck pond. Every spring, cherry blossom. Leafy, suburban. We were the noisy foreigners.

Thirteen days after Persian New year, *No-rooz,* we'd carry plates of wheatgrass down to the river and throw it in, to take the bad luck away, hoping no-one would notice or ask what we were doing. Little green islands floating towards the sea –

Wapping,

Greenwich,

Tilbury.

Five Poems

S A R A H   W H I T E

He Offers a Reason

'Because it was he, because it was I.'
Montaigne, 'On Friendship'

Lonely Montaigne, having had a perfect
confidant and lost him, decided to invent
the Essay as a way to touch his friend,
Etienne, again: He would wander from thought
to thought, as in their former conversations,
and simply let the Reader listen in.

As one such Reader, I say Merci, Michel,
for telling me, as well as any writer could,
a reason for your art. What
about my own? I won't go into that

until I've thanked you for combing through the Greek
and Latin classics, teasing out their wisdom,
and carving it into the roof beams of your library.
I like that gift to your visitors. I don't much like

your disdain for women, especially those
in your château, who spoke and wrote no Latin
in the garden or the kitchen, or in chambers
tending doomed blue infants, while the mind
of the *Seigneur* remained on his Book, with the King
himself awaiting a new edition!

Michel, you knew the King would soon
be gone. Likewise, the women and, alas,
the children. Nothing you could write
in classical or modern tongue
would touch them, even if they listened.

Nor will any lines of mine be wise or beautiful
enough to touch the souls I miss – friends, lovers, children.

At 'The Mount'

Edith Wharton's Mansion, Lenox, MA

In a flimsy of linens
I glimpse her Wish, washed,
rinsed, heat-treated –
a blast.

See the mahogany pantry:
To every shelf
its own sequester,
to every world
its own oyster.

Bon appétit!
Try the cottage cheese! Try
the prose: *I love you, babe,
more than my phone,
more than my parts
of speech.*

The soup
of the day surprises,
while an oval tray
offers its arc of snacks

Good-bye, Intelligent Design.

Good-bye, awful nick-name,
yours and mine the same—

Puss! it doesn't suit us.

The Art Spirit[1]

*Nobody wanted Walt Whitman but Walt Whitman
wanted himself.*

Seeing a tan and white pigeon
peck at a weed, a word, or a worm
on the walk in front of my building,
I conclude that the creature wouldn't be there
if Mother Pigeon were one
of those bird-brains who lays
her eggs on a slanted roof.
She must have wanted this pigeon
as much as it wanted itself.

---

1 *The Art Spirit*, a book of reflections by the painter
Robert Henri, 1865–1929.

Valediction On Shelving
Your Complete English Poems

Because your Sun was blinding,
light leaking through the cracks
in my Sleepers' Den,
because an awful knell was heard all over town,

I consigned your works and the portrait on the cover
to a cell so narrow that a common monk
might reside there instead of you, John Donne.

I muffled your momentous voice, built a wall
of books around the slot you're buried in,
bracelet and bone. Forgive me. Tell me

all is well and the niche is not too thin.
Tell me it's as wide as an Inn for the Guest
at a Prince's wedding or a Queen's beheading.

The Lay of the Honeysuckle

I die without you and you without me –
  like a vine torn from its tree.
Marie de France

Hers is a rhyme-rich tongue,
where tree and vine agree,
rich in limbs and tombs,
stems and puns –
*l'amour/la mors, le cuers
le cors* – heart and body hard
to tell apart – like you from me,
him from her, as if the tale
were an infant born
at sea – *la mer/la mère* –
an orphan, husband
in the shadow of the wrong
bride, the right name –
a sister to his friend, a friend
  to his wound as, in some far-off
land, the true Isolde
boards a ship, its white
sails blackened by a lie
as the hero dies.
Love failing, finding
one another's tomb
to touch in deep
distress, Tristesse, Tristan –
the man, the noun, the sound
of mortal harm.

The Year of Grey and other poems

KATHERINE LOCKTON

The Year of Grey

For Stephanie

The year of grey started with an elephant
I had been ignoring, in the corner of my room
blowing his trumpet till I could no longer ignore him.
I fed him carrots, beef stew leftovers
& sandwiches I stole from other people's bags.
I could no longer pretend he wasn't there
& that I didn't love or want him,
more that I wanted breath in my lungs.

The Rape Scene

How do you tell someone that they have been living
in the wrong house. That a home is not somewhere
you are scared to be and that not all men lie, use
and abuse. One day you will learn
that how you grew up was not like everyone else
and that there was never anything you could do.
You will learn that trauma is silent
and that there is no background music to a rape scene.

*

There is no special lighting in a rape scene.
The director hasn't spent hours fiddling
with undertones and fixtures.
Neither has the rapist. He is here.
There is a car with car seats
or the national theatre with the river
in the background. The place you used
to want to be married in, the place
your sister wanted to be married
which he has made a rape scene.

*

He tries to hold your hand in the café
you say *no* firmly, say that you are leaving
but he says sorry, he won't do it again.

*

He whispers in your ear while you dance
at his sister's wedding. Later your mother,
the woman who bought you into this world,
heard your first scream and your first heart
beat against hers, the woman you love,
will refer to that night as the night you got off
with the bride's brother.

*

Your cousin.
Your ex's friend.

*

Music is playing in his car. He is drunk and driving
you home. He pulls in
and you panic.

*

You ripped your dress so you wouldn't
have to go to the wedding. You sensed it,
the danger coming. Your angry mother
in the bathroom with your sister. You bang
on the door when he first gives you that look,
the I want to fuck you look. You tear
your dress. Your mother, annoyed hands you another.

*

He pulls his car in and you can already see
it happening as it happens because it does happen.

*

There is no music playing in the background
of the rape scene, even though there is
you can't hear it. You are somewhere else.

*

You ask yourself what is a rape anyway?
A finger? A mouth? A

*

After you say to yourself it must be your fault.
That it can't have happened. Not twice. Not to you.

*

How can it be his fault? He/they has/have a mother. A wife.
A daughter and son.

*

Your mother says it isn't rape because he is younger
than you. Did you rape him?

*

Why did you protect him? When people looked
why did you cover your eyes so they couldn't see
the pain? Why did you kiss his forehead,
the rapist's forehead, the next morning
as his mother looked on smiling as he slept
on your bed, still apparently drunk,
you suddenly sober from the truth.

*

Why did you kiss his forehead as he slept?

*

You shout and scream at him at the foot of the stairs.
He wants to hug you. You don't let him.
Instead you walk away. Get the bus home
and don't tell anyone. How can you?

*

You imagine your ex talking to him.
Then you realise you can never tell anyone.

*

And why did you 6 months later accuse
your father instead then hide in a mental hospital.
The only place you felt safe, the only place
you feel safe even now?

*

You see someone slit their neck with plastic.
But still this is better. To be safe. Here.

*

Why do you continue to protect him/them?

*

Because you don't want to create a scene.

A rape scene. With a white chalked outline
of your body. Now someone else's body.

Even though you said no or couldn't say no.

Even though you said no more times that night
than you have ever said yes in your life.

Being Alice

I wanted to be smaller
so I cut my paper dolls and me smaller
and smaller
but still they came for me
those girls who called me names and kicked

I wanted to be bigger
to kick back so I had seconds
ate bread
but then the men came

I started to shrink again
but the men

they came back
hungrier

and I realised
I had to stay me
I had to be who I already was

Light 'thick as honey among the grasses'

Two unpublished notebooks by R.S. Thomas

M. WYNN THOMAS

A FEW YEARS BACK I wrote as follows: 'There are deaths that have affected the very weather of the Welsh mind, and for two days after R.S. Thomas's passing in September, 2000, the country was swept by storms. What mattered to many, towards the end of his long life, was that he was still there, magnificently cussed, wilfully bloody-minded, incorrigibly anachronistic. In a world glib with yes-men his was a voice ever ready to say No! in thunder.'

His death burdened me with a heavy responsibility, as he had appointed me literary executor of his unpublished estate. In that capacity I first acted as custodian of such of his manuscripts as remained and then, in accordance with his express wishes, selected a handful of previously unpublished poems for publication. The resultant volume, *Residues*, appeared in 2002, after which Thomas's papers were transferred by me to his family, who sold them to the R. S. Thomas Research Centre at Bangor University. As for me, I turned to interpreting his poetry in the volume *R. S. Thomas: Serial Obsessive*, published to mark the hundredth anniversary of his birth. In due course, Professor Tony Brown and Professor Jason Walford Davies, the joint Directors of the R. S. Thomas Centre, brought out with Bloodaxe a collection of several new painting poems under the title *Too Brave to Dream*. But many other fine poems still remain unpublished.

I had supposed my duties concluded with the placement in safe keeping of what appeared to be all of Thomas's unpublished materials. However, a short time ago, a further set of papers, consisting of a sheaf of typescript poems and two Notebooks, came very unexpectedly to light. These are currently in my care, and I deem it in the best interests of enhancing Thomas's high reputation as a poet (a matter of particular concern to him, as he stressed when we discussed my duties as executor) to summarise a few illuminating highlights from the Notebooks here, after the following brief overview of their contents.

Notebook One (Nbk 1) has been partially filled both from the front and from the back. The former text consists primarily of relatively short journal entries, intermittent in character and covering the years from January, 1944 to June, 1945. These jottings include some that throw an arresting new light on Thomas's fundamental preoccupations. They are followed by quotations from some of the writers Thomas was reading at the time. The 'back' of the Notebook consists of notes on the antiquities associated with many of the villages of Montgomeryshire and the March that neighboured Thomas's parish of Manafon (Llandysilio, Carno, Llanfyllin, Llansantffraed, Llanymynach, Llandrinio, Montgomery etc.). These are followed by a detailed, lengthy summary of the history of Ireland,

a country Thomas had visited and to which he was, at this relatively early juncture, still very strongly attracted. There is also a sheaf of loose-leaf insertions, consisting of long reading lists, headings for sermons, and more notes on Ireland, this time written in Welsh.

Notebook Two (Nbk 2) has likewise been filled from two directions. What seems to have been the 'front' consists of a few pages of nature jottings from the year 1946, followed by a scattering of prayers and meditations, mostly relating to the priestly office of the laying on of hands to heal the sick. As for the 'back,' it contains summaries, one or two of which are very detailed, of the many books Thomas was assiduously reading in the early 1950s. These entries are likely to prove very fertile territory for anyone interested in the development during this period of the poet's outlook on theology (including eco-theology), the creative process, culture, history, and science. Before concluding, the following discussion will therefore also aim to supply some preliminary examples of this.

*

A recurrent interest in the diaries is in the movement of birds. Thus on Whit Sunday, 1944, we learn of 'A day of excessive heat following a smearing of ground frost on the grass in the low meadows. In the middle of the day the heron stood in Cae Siencyn, like a voluminous umbrella in a stand.....The flies in the wood tonight so thick that it was like riding through showers of sand.' (Nbk1, May 28, 1944) Thomas repeatedly restricts himself to the faithful discipline of minutely noting his immediate environment, seeing himself as a latter-day Gilbert White or Thomas Hardy, and wondering whether this might not be the 'sign of achievement in a writer – to make his own district interesting and desirable even as his characters?'

Months later, he is confessing that 'I turn to the land for healing, and always I am healed. Up into the moors beyond Cefn Coch today. Clean wind, sharp night edged sky and dark, damp moors. Always they comfort and strengthen and purify. Strip the soul to their simple strength and what would there be to fear. All the things in the field are my neighbours, and yet too often to be thought of only when missed.' Calling to mind the rare, sacred moments when 'every blade of grass, every leaf, every flower becomes dear and terrible,' he reminds himself that 'These are my material, my subjects for study and of them and my relation to them I must have strength to write. Though the world will not listen. 'For thou shall be in league with the stones of the field, and the beasts of the field shalt be at peace with thee.' Stone and bone, skull and flower – is there a difference?' (Nbk1, Oct 19, 1944)

More than a year was to pass before he published his important first volume, duly entitled *Stones of the Field,* the title to the volume taken, like the epigraph, from the Book of Job. And in the February of 1945 it was of that very same 'eternal masterpiece' he had been reminded when wrestling with the suffering everywhere evident in what otherwise could be a ravishingly beautiful natural environment. He found temporary consolation by reflecting that by 'remembering the flower blushing unseen, and the impersonal of the great frost, one cannot avoid the thought again that compared with such a superlative God human suffering is no more than very, very relative importance tragic as it may seem.' (Nbk1,Feb 14, 1945) It was, however, a conclusion with which he could never rest satisfied for long. Moreover, in another astonishingly unexpected moment of self-knowledge, he briefly doubts even the sufficiency for his personal needs of his customary devotion to nature. 'I ask myself am I right to concentrate on the earth and nature as I do,' he wonders disconcertingly. 'At times it seems so right, and in the heyday of the blood there is nothing I would not tackle, nowhere I would not live, and it be close to the stones and grasses but one thing is certain, this is not wholly me, or if it is demands all my courage to sustain it. Because ever and anon I see it as an unprofitable waste, or as a grim field of battle, all of which suggests that I am sick or abnormal, and there is nothing in Nature for the sick or the abnormal.' (Nbk1, Feb , 1945)

More typical is his celebration of 'the time of year that is sweetest when the grasses are thronged with flowers, cowparsley and daisies, buttercups and clover, bluebells and orchis [sic], where the bee loses his way and the willow warbler lives.' (Nbk1, June 2, 1944) Such lyrical exclamations punctuate his text, as when he marvels at the evening sunlight, 'thick as honey among the grasses.' Instinctive poet that he knows himself to be, he immediately recognizes in such moments that here 'are words and phrases lying ready to hand,' before thoughtfully adding 'but what shall I make of them.' (Nbk1, June 11, 1944) And he can register the phases of the day with the same delicacy with which he marks the passing of the seasons: 'In the late evening the sun spins a web of silver in the fir trees before my window. Sun, sun, that strokes my flesh and touches me tenderly as a giant touches a bird, one day you will peer under my lids and recoil at the darkness.' (Nbk1, June 9, 1944)

That late modulation, during the course of a single sentence, from what starts out as an ecstasy of sensuous experience into the plangency of melancholy is another recurrent characteristic of 'nature' observations that readily incline towards reflections, often sombre or lugubrious, on the human condition. Envying the total unself-conscious absorption of a greenfinch in the simple business of living, he knows himself humanly haunted by such questions as 'What is life, what is consciousness, what is immortality,' and regretfully accepts that he can share the earth with the bird 'only in idea, [and] that she shares with me only sensually.' (Nbk1, May 29, 1944) In the drumming hooves of restless cattle agitated by flies in the summer heat he hears 'an echo of the world's trouble.' After noticing 'the sea greying for rain and the first larks singing above y maes pridd,' he can't resist adding 'A lark sings above the dying man.' (Nbk2, Jan.29,

1946) Similarly, he records 'A wild night of wind and rain and now the river over its banks and the dark surly water into the roads and the field, and a thrush singing over the waste of it,' before adding a coda: 'A bird singing over the ruins of the world.' (Nbk. 2, Feb 8, 1946).

Such entries are no doubt indirect responses to the post-war devastation of Europe. His corresponding awareness that his country parish affords him refuge during a time of the breaking of nations is memorably acknowledged on June 6, 1944, when he writes: 'Today the British and American forces landed again in France and a great slaughter was begun. But here in the country all things remain as before....This is how war always has been in the country districts – nothing more than a rumour beyond the last hedge top.'

The panic caused among the smaller birds by the mere arrival of a magpie on the lawn reminds him, however, that 'Man then is not the only disturber of nature.' And throughout his diary he agonizes over the dilemma of how to reconcile the savage violence that is secretly alive all around him in the quiet fields and woods with the beauty of the world by which he is often overwhelmed; 'Up beyond the Gweunydd this evening. So happy to be wandering the lanes, the wind, tides of wind in the boughs and the hurrying clouds above. I kneel clasping my staff – and I am. All the universe leads up and centres itself in me. This is not pride but a sweet humility.' (Nbk1, June 14, 1944)

It is the 'inexorableness of nature's laws' that implacably confronts him with the most insoluble paradox of all: 'I say love is one of the highest, if not the highest, things we know – it is creative, it is space-straining, time-mastering, but God is not love. It is a partial truth, or a failure of terminology, or the result of a misconception of the nature of deity. To hold it is to encounter insoluble problems, irreconcilable facts.' (Nbk1, June 15, 1944) At the very beginning of 1945 he writes of 'Snow on the land and bitter frost at night and everywhere signs of the unceasing struggle. Not only in France, China and Russia, but here also there is war, relentless, unbroken war, blood on the snow and feathers and festering bones.' (Nbk1, Jan. 23, 1945)

The D-Day landings may in one sense have seemed remote from Manafon experience for Thomas, but in another there is no doubt that background awareness of them greatly heightened his sensitivity to violent suffering in his immediate surroundings. Finding a young rabbit lying in shock on the ground where an owl had dropped it, and seeing it bleeding from the mouth, he feels compelled to put it out of its pain, and so dispatches it with two hammer blows on the head. This leads to an agony of self-recrimination: 'Violence appals me, therefore I will not resort to it if I can help it. I will never acquiesce in war or in the law of nature say what they will. "Poetry is not made by fertile blood" they say and I am a poet – but poetry is *one* aspect of truth.'

Each outcry of the hunted hare
A fibre from the main doth tear.

The trouble with contemporary life is that we have all become withdrawn from realities. It is a far cry from the potted meat on our table to the bleeding creature. Men are killed in southern England now by others who press a lever in France. It needs thought and imagination now to realize the full import of Abel's blood crying from the ground. The average man has neither – 'wise in his own conceit.' Life is a tragedy also to those who think, but whereas none can avoid feeling, most people have long-ago been taught not to think too much.' (Nbk1, June 25, 1944)

A fortnight later, and he is still brooding on his feelings about 'the average man,' feelings he bleakly acknowledges to be so full of 'hatred' (his own frank term) as to disqualify him from being a true Christian. 'There are so many that I come near to hating when I see them or hear them or hear about them – it is their meanness that I hate, their meanness and complacency, and most of all I hate the clergy, for of all men they are the most complacent. I do not know one single one of them that comes anywhere near to being the fine, deep man that he should be.' This leads to an exasperated exclamation: 'ah! I am not a Christian at heart, but rather an artist, with something of the artist's arrogance maybe for I despise these ill-bred, mean, complacent, conceited creatures among whom I have been tonight.' (Nbk1, July 14, 1944)

*

This recognition that he is first and foremost a poet is one with which Thomas continues to struggle thereafter, and, as we shall see, it leads him to range far and wide intellectually in his reading in a dogged attempt to improve his understanding of how to reconcile his calling as a Christian with his poetic vocation. A related dilemma is that of his relationship to language, one aggravated by his growing devotion to Welsh. 'I have tried and tried,' he records in July 29, 1944, 'to arouse within myself sufficient enthusiasm to contemplate life as a Welsh speaking parson. I have returned again and again to the language as a moth to the candle – But oh, my language of expression – my medium of speech is English, and for the hundredth time I discover that without writing poetry I cannot live, I cannot live.' (Nbk1, July 29, 1944) This must surely be one of the most crucial *cris de coeur* ever to have been committed to paper by Thomas.

The diary similarly lays bare his fear of death. The night of 22 October 1944, he lies 'awake my nose clogged by a clod and that old enemy of mine came near, so that I grew nervous and restless, and the sweet voiced river grew sullen and threatening. "Confusion of the deathbed." [The phrase is from 'A Cold Heaven,' by Yeats.] That's the trouble. I see all things as shadows of that final feeling of suffocation and confusion and knowing my nervousness now, ask what of that day or night?' His fear is aggravated by his piercing awareness that one day he will have to leave the beauty of the natural world behind for ever. 'I need courage. I need strength and where shall I find it in the dark hours, with no moon, no stars, but in thee, O God.?'

And then, as if as a postscript, he adds a moving touch of mortal solidarity, when he writes 'I saw her [presumably his wife Mildred Eldridge] coming through the brittle day carrying a branch of coloured leaves, that burned like a torch.' It is as if he were glimpsing Persephone, returned from the realm of the dead with all the bounty not of spring but of late autumn in her arms. Elsewhere, too, autumn assumes a benign aspect for

him: 'I always say that November and December are maligned. Tforhey can show as fair a day as any in the year. Today after night frost the sky changed to an archipelago of soft grey cloud, which again yielded to a sea of blue, and all the twigs shone in the sun. The today which only autumn knows, like the peace of strong hands after their work is done.' (Nbk1, Nov. 16, 1944) But such ruminations can nevertheless be immediately followed by contrary observations: 'The young dark buds on the branch are like a beast's claws, and after all do not the trees themselves hold the earth with their roots, as a hawk grasps its prey? "I am sick, I must die, / Lord have mercy on us."' (Nbk1, Nov 19, 1944)

*

There is one moment reminiscent of Jung's action, when a child, of keeping a ruler he'd carved into a tiny mannequin, along with a painted stone, in a pencil case secreted in his attic. It was an action he later believed had been taken by a lonely child intent on safeguarding his secret 'other,' 'inner,' 'true' self, a being utterly distinct from his ordinary quotidian personality. In reflecting on the 'knowledge that is peculiar to oneself and that will be spilled like water when the pitcher is broken at the fountain,' Thomas adds: 'who knows but I that somewhere under the green turf of Llechrydau there is a box buried containing petals?' (Nbk1, December 6, 1944)

December 8th, 1944 finds him transported by the quiet beauty of a snowy countryside, 'the light... silver and all... fresh as a bubble. The light splintered like glass...The birds glitter like whitebait against the black sky.' Suddenly he is overwhelmed by 'the sympathy of God. Perhaps even with me he is not entirely out of sympathy, this patient God, who else brought me to this place of hills and a river and uncouth men and sweaty women? Even with my need to be broken and blasted like a tree, to root deep in the earth, to lose all but a leaf's yearning for the sky. Even with this perhaps he has patience. The terrible clarity of Virginia Woolf and it broke her. But it shall not break me, for I shall keep one foot deep in the earth. Beauty shall craze me, pain bewilder, the meanness of men turn a knife in my heart, but though to the world I am dry and useless as a rotting tree, within the sap shall rise again, my speech bud and glitter anew. If the sap enter the veins, the mind will not crumble.'

This experience culminates in a kind of epithalamium: a celebration of the mystical marriage between him and the natural world, and between him and the wife who is his soul companion. 'Forgive me, O Lord God,' he writes: 'I wish nothing more of heaven than what I have seen today. All the morning I was from window to window because of the moving pageant of the sky, the quality of the light that would crumble at the hands' touch, and in the afternoon walking to Rhiwhiriaeth with her who is most dear, what more could I ever need? I was in no pain, yet gloriously alive, gloriously conscious of the clear air, the intense colour. The far hills, sailing ships of snow, and we walked on the edge of a black cloud, ourselves "riddled with light".' That last is of course another quotation from Yeats's famous sonnet 'The Cold Heaven.'

And as he further reflects a day later, only spiritual belief could enable a person truly to face up to the harsh realities of the human condition. Most people, he believed, 'are extroverted... to something that saves them from themselves. It needs a sacred soul to face itself in the mirror of solitude and modern life heaps up those external props without which a man is lost. Virginia Woolf saw this and it was surely another cause of her suicide.' (Nbk1, Dec. 9, 1944)

There are moments, too, when Thomas recognizes his reliance on particular places that for him constitute 'home.' January 29, 1945 turns out to be for him 'A day of nostalgia, though whether of place or time I could not say. Holyhead – always there, though not always consciously so – will suddenly rise before me in all its fresh, windy beauty, and I see again so clearly the dear roads that lead to the sea and the dewy grass and the flying foam, so that I feel an exile here amid these inland fields which yet are fair. On days such as these I cannot think straight at all, but must needs yield to my emotion, until all I want is the sea, the sea! Yet not any sea either, but that which breaks on the coast where the plovers used to rest, and the gorse warmed the air. Where I would sometimes count myself blessed because I had found the first violets or met Flora and Isabel walking in the lanes.' (Nbk1, 1945)

Equally memorable is an extended passage recorded on March 2, 1945:

> To South Wales by train to get the feel of the country – but oh, I belong to North Wales. There are mountains and lakes there and birds and sheep, but they might have been the North of England for all they mean to me. What strange spell is this upon me, that if I go anywhere in North Wales, Talyllyn, Lleyn, Anglesey, Llangurig, I feel at home. Whereas nowhere in the wide world else will I have that feeling. Is it that my mind has been formed out of things which are essentially North-Welsh? I know that when I hear or read the word water I see a "pistyll" somewhere in Merioneth, or if valley a "glyn," and pass a bwlch such as around Llangywer. It is no use – I am powerless against it. I have tried to be noble and to say "Wherever God calls me, there I will go," but if He called to the South or to England, I could not obey. It seems awful that soul should be stronger than spirit in me, but thus it seems. I am hearing ever the strange accent or inflection of a pennillion [sic] singer, and seeing with most pleasure the keen dark face of a Merioneth shepherd.' (Nbk1)

Thomas never was to venture long or far into the 'foreign' territory of South Wales, although he may never have felt wholly comfortable either with being confined to a particular region. Indeed a mere week later than his extended entry we find him chiding himself 'that a person cannot be like that. He cannot give way to his emotional life, because it is too vulnerable a thing. To be emotional is to be weak. That is the hard fact, and there is no room in the world for weak things. If I yield to the earth and be like it, then I become vulnerable. If I ally myself with it – I cannot face the problems either of the world or the Spirit.' However, rebuke himself as he may, he ends up conceding that 'I am an artist and the true artist does ally himself with the world and so becomes vulnerable – but what when he is a priest?' (Nbk1, March 8, 1945)

At much the same time, he also faced up to another of what he regarded as the chronic weaknesses of his nature when he asked 'Whence comes the furtive love of death within one. The flirtation with destruction, evil, annihilation...At times as I read or think of the future, I realize how little love I have for spiritual health and perfection, as compared with the darker waywardness of the soul. It is only in moments of weakness or sickness of body that [I] run whimpering to a God created out of my immediate need. Well, I see God as spirit, moving endless, impersonal as wind, through the waste places of the world.' (Nbk1, March 14, 1945)

Nor was he unaware that in Mildred Eldridge he had chosen a wife of like temperament to himself, as becomes apparent in an entry of March 12, 1945:

> Today I gave her a white violet for her hair as a pledge of what we will one day do. For we know that we will never grow old in the Church, never grow comfortable and tolerant of other people, never make our peace with the world. The older we get, the less we will stomach the people around us, the more saeva indignatio will rend us. Deep in our hearts is the desire to go away somewhere where nature is still untroubled, "untainted by man's misery." It is the return of the native to the sea, sepulture and sunset of West Britain. (Nbk1, March 12, 1945)

That turned out to be, indeed, a profoundly prophetic passage.

On May 7th, 1945, Thomas laconically reported that 'Peace of a formal nature has returned to Europe with the signing of an armistice between Germany and the Allies.' One cannot, however, escape the feeling that another development, recorded a month or so later, was of much greater moment in his own life. 'I have begun to write again,' he there notes with unmistakeable relief: 'only a song – but the real thing. Full circle through the weary business of being to the only worthwhile becoming.' (Nbk1, June 15, 1945) Interestingly enough it is the concluding entry in the diary, as if it had served its purpose in enabling the return of his poetic gifts.

He had sensed such a recovery of his psychic and poetic powers a couple of months earlier. 'So,' he wrote in March 17, 1945, 'by many a devious and meandering path, I come again to myself. The vessel sings though empty, if the wind pass over it. But I must overflow before song is born of me. Ideas alone waken the true lyrical impulse. Is it because without reading I am so empty that I fail to sing? Yes.' (Nbk1) This for Thomas is an exceedingly rare moment, when he reflects on the secret sources of his poetry, and what is noteworthy is that at this crucial juncture he specifically chooses to discard the traditional Romantic image of the wind as the carrier of divine inspiration in favour of a very different image – very unfashionable and supposedly 'prosaic' – of books and reading.

*

This revelatory entry highlights for us one fundamental aspect of Thomas's poetry that has been consistently overlooked by critics. From the very beginning, and not only in its late phase, it was every bit as much a 'poetry of ideas' as it was a 'poetry of nature.' Ideas not only provided him with raw materials, they proved to be the best stimulus for his writing. No wonder that he adhered throughout his mature life to the rigid discipline of reserving every morning whenever possible for reading, before venturing abroad after lunch.

It is therefore unfortunate that we know so little about the books Thomas read – even the tiny library he had with him at the end was cavalierly dispersed immediately after his passing, although such of it as could be saved is now safely housed in the R.S. Thomas Centre. The notes, some of them very detailed, he made on around two dozen books he was reading around the mid-1950s are accordingly a rarity and correspondingly of immense potential value. They bring to our attention the thinking of a range of authors whose possible influence on Thomas has not hitherto been suspected or, therefore, explored. All the quotations that follow are taken from his second Notebook, unless otherwise indicated.

There was one book in particular that he chose to summarise in very great detail. This was *Christ and Culture*, published in 1951 by the eminent American theologian Richard Niebuhr, and it basically considered two contrasting views taken by theologians of the relationship of Christianity to the contemporary world. One school, most brilliantly represented by the great, uncompromisingly Evangelical, German theologian Karl Barth, concentrated on Christ's announcement that his kingdom was not of this world. Accordingly, the members of this school insisted, albeit to varying degrees, that there was necessarily a great schism between Christianity and 'culture.' Those 'liberals' of an opposite persuasion (including Niebuhr), although all again of somewhat different views, tended to emphasise the risen Christ's transforming presence *in* the world.

Thomas expresses no view as to his own position, but his choice of further reading, combined with his constant struggle to reconcile his faith, and his trust in love, with the harsh, frequently cruel, realities of both the social and the natural order, strongly suggest that he favoured Niebuhr's extremely challenging outlook. One of the more unorthodox thinkers along these lines whose work interested him was Canon C. E. Raven, sometime Regius Professor of Divinity at Cambridge. His adoption of a spiritually purposive evolutionary theory owing more to Lamarck and Pierre de Chardin than to Charles Darwin clearly appealed to a Thomas constantly tortured by the antinomies of nature. From his reading of Raven's 1943 series of eight lectures on 'Science, Religion and the Future,' Thomas selected the tentative observation that 'With the active assistance of God's indwelling spirit the creation gropes its way forward in hope,' and he implicitly approved Raven's authoritative statement that 'We shall not see a return to the Old orthodoxies: 3 centuries of scientific study have profoundly altered our whole understanding of the order of nature.' Thomas went so far as to add to this a note from himself to remember Herbert Read's dictum that future poetry would be more scientific, while later, no doubt ruefully, picking out a comment by Raven that 'a poet with the necessary knowledge in science, history, philosophy and religion would be hard to find.'

Thomas also glossed Raven's positive vision of an evolving universe by remarking that it seemed to him the 'Idea of nature as a growing changing or living work of art instead of a finished work by [an] outside maker' was 'more in keeping with modern thought and allows for redemption of nature – cf Isaiah's vision.' It was probably this line of thinking that led him to study A. N. Whitehead's *Science and the Modern World*. A highly influential work first published in 1925, it continues to this day to be regarded as one of the foundational text both of eco-theology and of process theology – contemporary modes of Christian thinking whose relevance to Thomas's religious poetry might well prove fruitful to consider. Another early proponent of process theology was Archbishop William Temple, from whose Gifford Lectures, published in 1934 under the title *Nature, Man & God*, Thomas isolates the sentence that 'The only way to hold together a vital religion and a scientific apprehension of the world is to assert some form of Divine Immanence.' He also consulted *Christian Theology and Natural Science,* a volume published in 1956 by the major Anglo-Catholic theologian E.L. Mascall.

Thomas's cognate thoughts about the relationship of modern science to Christian beliefs led him, during the mid-1950s, to consult the writings of such authors as J. G. Bennett, whose 1956 volume *The Dramatic Universe* betrayed an interest in the thinking of Gurdjeff. Others of like venturesome inclinations whose work is mentioned in the Notebook are C. E. M. Joad and Arthur Koestler, from whose *Insight and Culture* (1949) Thomas took a perception that was to shape his future thinking about 'the Machine': 'Technical products isolate man from nature not artificial per se but his lack of understanding of science disconnects his environment from universal order.' At much the same time, Thomas was dabbling in works exploring the depths of selfhood, such as *God and the Unconscious* (1953) by Victor White, a Dominican priest who was a very close, if independently minded and critical, friend of Carl Jung.

*

One subject that was naturally of very particular interest to Thomas, both as priest and as poet, was that of language, especially in its relation to spiritual reality. The Notebook alerts us to Thomas's reading on this matter in the work of several authors whose thought has hitherto never been connected with his writing. One such is the prominent Anglican Canon and scholar, F.W. Dillistone, whose many books published over a very long lifetime included *Christianity and Symbolism* (1955), *The Power of Symbols* (1975), *Traditional Symbols and the Contemporary World* (1973), *The power of Symbols in Religions and Culture* (1986), *Christianity and Symbolism*, and *Myth and Symbol.* Of these, only the first had appeared at the time that Thomas was engaging with his thinking, but all of Dillistone's publications seem to have been predicated on an assumption cognate with that stated by Thomas Mann, which was quoted in his later work: 'To live symbolically spells true freedom.'

Thomas's brief series of notes on his reading in Dillistone include several remarks revealing of his own poetic practice. So he emphasises that 'According to Dillistone – fossilisation of symbols can be prevented by rigorous use of analogical method. This allows for rapprochement between Christianity & mechanism so my assocn. of Christianity & nature can only be saved from fossilisation by remembering that "there lives the dearest freshness deep down things." (G[erard] M[anley] Hopkins).' In another jotting he adds a reminder to himself: 'NB metaphor – dep on creative individual.' He also pointedly underlines the relevance of another Dillistone observation: 'NB Dillistone's reference to non-conformer's part in breaking the stereotyped pattern leading to fossilisation cf the sudden change in a dance rhythm. So in Christian worship.' And then there is a further, mournful, note to himself: 'NB Slow rate of change in old societies compared with speed of change today/ No time for modern symbol to acquire depth and penetration.' Thomas was clearly very interested in the kind of thinking about symbols that had emanated from the work of Ernst Cassirer, and his Notebook includes a reference to Susanne K. Langer's important *Feeling and Form*, first published in 1953.

Equally suggestive is the very brief mention by Thomas of *The Tyranny of Words* by the American economist Stuart Chase, who was a follower of the socialist philosophy of Thorsten Veblen. The book was a popularisation of Alfred Korzybski's theory of general semantics, central to which was the contention that since language is a purely human device, it is reflective of the characteristics of the human brain and of limited use accordingly. By definition it can provide no access to absolute reality. Korzybski's most pithy dictum was that 'The map is not the territory.' Thomas notes that Chase 'quotes Malinowski, in support of the theory that thought is influenced by accepted structure of language more than language is influenced by reflection. This is my old theory about vocabulary influencing history. NB The danger of accepting an increasingly authoritative scientific vocabulary. This too à propos – religion poetry and modern life.'

Finally, towards its conclusion, this section of the Notebook shows us Thomas constantly worrying about how far Christianity can be reconciled with poetry. A recurrent concern is that the former may make demands of the latter that are detrimental to the production of authentic poetry. Repeatedly faced with this concern, Thomas with equal stubbornness insists that the only enemy of poetry is not Christian faith per se but Christian dogma: 'I think the pressure of Christianity on the freedom of the artist comes from individual texts, or intreptns, by religious groups of certain aspects of Christianity rather than from "Jesus Himself."' Hymns Ancient and Modern, he insists, are 'not weak because about Xty but because weak *poets.*' He responds to the assertion that 'Since the Reformation, none of the English major poets have written as Christians,' with a laconic query: 'T.S. Eliot?' And on occasion he ventures even further, such as when he confidently states that 'Philosophically a strong case can be made out for a Christian prequirement to all art,' or wonders 'Will not Xtn. poet give true value to evil etc in order to increase the impact of his total message whereas a poet with evil intent cannot allow virtue much scope – consequently his work in a small scale.'

'When I was young,' he recalls, 'I subscribed to the common view of Christianity's effect on poetry. As one grows older it is to the conception of that service which is perfect freedom that one strives to grow.' After all, 'Of many attempts to find a coherent & comprehensive system – Christianity most impressive therefore should be possible for arts to exist within it.' This was the faith, very difficult though he may have found it to maintain, that was to sustain him, as poet and priest, right to the very end. As he had prophetically written almost sixty years before his death: 'It seems as if his own peculiar problem must haunt each man all his life to remain unsolved even as his eyes close.' (Nbk1, May 28, 1944)

From the Archive

Issue 151, May–June 2003

MARILYN HACKER

Fellow contributors to this issue include David Kinloch, Edwin Morgan, Alison Brackenbury, Robert Minhinnick and Neil Powell.

A SUNDAY AFTER EASTER

A child who thought departure would be sweet,
I roam the borders of my neighbourhood
dominical, diminished. Young gay men
their elbows brushing, Sunday-stroll, in pairs
on their way to the weekend flea-market
on the boulevard Richard-Lenoir
at Oberkampf. I sit in a café
nursing a decaf. A small Chinese boy
(or girl) in sweats stands on tiptoes to reach
the flippers of the 'Space Pirates' machine.
I want to find some left turn into dream
or narrative, next chapter, memory
not saturated with regret, into
a vision as unlikely as the mare [...]

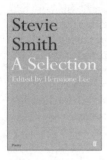

How do you know your Bog is dood?

Stevie Smith, *A Selection* (Faber) £12.99; Kathleen Raine, *Collected Poems* (Faber) £20

Reviewed by VALERIE DUFF-STRAUTMANN

The reissue from Faber of Kathleen Raine's and Stevie Smith's work brings back two voices that otherwise might be eclipsed by the ever-expanding volume occupied by contemporary poetry. In addition, both women, very influential in their own time, though completely different in aesthetic, are largely absent from the great male canon of the twentieth century; each, however, left her notch. An avid reader wonders how they have fallen from conversation, but we can speculate: Stevie Smith is easy to dismiss as a light versifier if you're not paying attention to her thrust; Kathleen Raine is likely known more for her scholarship of Yeats and Blake than for the 330 plus original poems (by Faber's count) she crafted for nearly a century. But Faber and Faber has restored them.

Stevie Smith: A Selection is reissued with the still-brilliant introduction by biographer and critic Hermione Lee that accompanied its first publication in 1983, a little over a decade after Smith's death. In the eighties, Smith's popularity was rising alongside feminist movements, and perhaps, in conjunction with late century expressions of cynicism. In life, Smith was uninterested in her contemporaries; as Lee points out, she was 'one of a generation which learned poetry by heart at school, and which knew the Bible and the Classics well, [her] mind...a "rag bag" of quotations.' She reached back deep and far, to Tennyson, Browning, Coleridge, Euripides, and Seneca for lessons in craft. She was also disinterested in following any literary club or formula, if any would have invited her in, but insisted on her own subjects and mannerisms, her own style, right down to how it all appeared in print (her doodles were to be printed with poems they accompanied, and were not--as Smith was not--to be dismissed).

'More than direct translation or quotation, she likes half-echoes, reminders, reworkings, travesties,' writes Lee of Smith in her introduction. Her poems can be brief, and her 'If I Lie Down' is simply this: 'If I lie down upon my bed I must be here,/But if I lie down in my grave I may be elsewhere' which, upon careful consideration, holds in its two lines echoes of the playful corrosiveness found in Shakespeare's Mercutio: 'Ask for me tomorrow and you shall find me a grave man.' One hears Blakean syncopation and earnestness in the seeming-silliness of 'Our Bog is Dood,' but here and elsewhere Smith holds herself outside the very pseudo-serious Christian drama:

> Our Bog is dood, our Bog is dood,
> They lisped in accents mild,
> But when I asked them to explain
> They grew a little wild.
> How do you know your Bog is dood

My darling little child?

> We know because we wish it so
> That is enough, they cried,
> And straight within each infant eye
> Stood up the flame of pride,
> And if you do not think it so
> You shall be crucified.

In the last stanza of 'Our Bog is Dood' she is alone. Smith keeps her distance from that water, and from the bickering children she speaks to, climbing the ever-so-logical contentment of 'sweet, sweeter, sweetest' as she removes herself from the hubbub of the nonsensical dood bog:

> Oh sweet it was to leave them then,
> And sweeter not to see,
> And sweetest of all to walk alone
> Beside the encroaching sea,
> The sea that soon should drown them all,
> That never yet drowned me.

It's not quite apostasy, but Smith holds firm in her disillusion.

Faber cuts a wide swath in *Stevie Smith: A Selection*, with writing from her opening salvo in 1936 to work published shortly before her death in 1972. *A Selection* is not just a selection of poems, because Stevie Smith was not just a poet; Smith's first publication was *Novel on Yellow Paper*, and she continued to write prose in addition to her highly musical verse. She proved ambidextrous, like Thomas Hardy and Emily Brontë before her, exploring satire, relationships, political perspective, and religious doubt, figuring out where the rules of poetry and prose diverge and where they could be made to overlap. The lines in her excerpted novels are a breathless stream-of-consciousness, such as these from *The Holiday*:

> My sister was not always so happy in her schools. In her last school, it was in Wales, it was like a madhouse. There it was a mixed boy-girl school, with a young, diffident and obstinate headmaster. He thought that to do the wrong thing strongly is better than to do nothing, but only he was by nature so vacillating that he could not even make up his mind what was the wrong thing, but if he was not impeded by a rationalizing attempt, he would do the wrong thing with a splendid spontaneity.

Smith reaches further into her toolbox for the imagery that completes this passage, in sentences as tightly wound as her briefest poems: 'The female sub-head in this school was a super thyroid who screamed and cried and made everybody so nervous. When the poor child was sick, she said, 'You cannot be sick here.' But where could he be sick? He was driven into the cold playground where the rain fell.'

Thinking of the old Virginia Slims ad, *You've come a long way, Baby*, I wonder if new poets, particularly female-identified poets, still consider trailblazers like Stevie Smith, who managed to be smart and funny, modern yet a virtuoso in channeling her predecessors, and she is nothing if not wickedly odd. Lee writes in her intro, 'The paradox of her art is that it is at once so allusive and so idiosyncratic,' and one finds examples of this paradox running rampant through *A Selection*. One senses that despite the weight of religion, society, gender rules, and whatever else life flung at her, Stevie Smith was trying to have *fun* when she took it on. For some poems, no doodles are necessary (this, from 'The River God'):

> I may be smelly and I may be old,
> Rough in my pebbles, reddy in my pools,
> But where my fish float by I bless their swimming
> And I like the people to bathe in me, especially women.
> But I can drown the fools
> Who bathe too close to the weir, contrary to rules.
> And they take a long time drowning
> As I throw them up now and then in a spirit of clowning.
> Hi yih, yippity-yap, merrily I flow,
> O I may be an old foul river but I have plenty of go.

Like Smith, Kathleen Raine's reissued *Collected Poems,* covers a prolific writing life that spanned over half a century of publications, beginning in 1943 and ending with poems dated 1999. Like Smith, in the Raine's *Collected*, one hears the writer's unmistakable voice, but unlike Smith, Raine's gravitas is what holds this collection together. Kathleen Raine outlines her principles and explains how she envisions being remembered for her body of work:

> Believing as I do, with my Master, William Blake, that 'One Power alone makes a poet -- Imagination, The Divine Vision': and with Yeats sharing his respect for the Vedic and Upanishadic tradition for which, as he saw them in Tagore, 'poetry and religion are the same thing'; it is in the light of this perennial wisdom that I would wish my work to be judged.

Her forms and content, over six decades, inevitably shift, but the soul is always present or longed for. There is the pure Yeatsian spirit, lonely and fulfilled in 'Northumbrian Sequence' (1952): 'Pure I was before the world began, / I was the violence of wind and wave, / I was the bird before bird ever sang. // I was never still, / I turned upon the axis of my joy, / I was the lonely dancer on the hill.' Remembrance and grief of those lost is immediate and palpable in 'The Wilderness' from 1965: 'The great ash long dead by a roofless house, its branches rotten, / The voice of the crows an inarticulate cry, / And from the wells and springs the holy water ebbed away. // A child I ran in the wind on a withered moor / Crying out after those great presences who were not there, / Long lost in the forgetfulness of the forgotten.' In the 1990s, with her death becoming more of a reality, she begins to shift perspective and moves into more personal exploration, in poems like 'I See My Little Cat,' here in full:

> I see my little cat sleeping in her favourite chair,
> Her world unquestioned and secure,
> And know I will be gone, and wonder where
> She will find a different chair, and will she remember
> The games we played: 'Is pussy coming to bed?' and 'Scamper-scamper!'
> And dashing before me to behind the bedroom door
> Hidden and crouching ready to pounce
> When my slow steps arrive, and I say 'Well done
> Little pussy!' and give her her supper on a saucer
> While I turn down my bed; and our morning play
> 'Come, pussy, down the garden!' and watch her tear
> Up the acacia tree where the pigeons are
> And a squirrel sometimes, and wonder whether
> She will remember my voice, and wonder
> Why her world has disappeared, or with nimble paws
> Leap lightly from here to there, secure.
> I hope she will not mourn me, or not for long.

Throughout, Raine's writing exudes the brilliance of what she's read. This is not at all unpleasant, and despite the weight her verse often carries, there are singular revelations that no Blake and no Yeats could provide authentically, despite the cover and expertise of metaphor ('I Felt, Under My Old Breasts'):

> I felt, under my old breasts, this April day,
> Young breasts, like leaf and flower to come, under grey apple buds
> And heard a young girl within me say,
> 'Let me be free of this winter bark, this toil-worn body,
> I who am young,
> My form subtle as a dream.'
> And I replied, 'You, who are I,
> Entered a sad house when you put on my clay.
> This shabby menial self, and life-long time,
> Bear with as you may
> Until your ripening joy
> Put off the dust and ashes that I am,
> Like winter scales cast from the living tree.'

Time and renewal, nature and the soul, are her subjects; these poems, Raine acknowledges are 'only one aspect of the imaginative adventure of my life... I could wish that my poetry might be read in the context of the whole scope of my life-work in the learning of the Imagination.' The life work of the poetry is neatly wrapped within this comprehensive *Collected*, illustrating, as Raine writes: 'To be is to be always here and now./The green linnet flits from bough to bough,' and her subjects and style underscore the desire she reveals in her forward: 'Better to be a little fish in the great ocean than to be a big fish in some literary rock-pool.'

As these are books reissued, one wonders what, in the world today, brings us around to these two at this moment in time? There have been no significant alterations to either volume, and the work of Kathleen Raine is nothing like the work of Stevie Smith. So one is left to wonder at the choice for and the timing of these releases.

Interestingly, one of the largest celebrations of the works of William Blake was exhibited this fall at the Tate Britain Gallery. While circumstantial, their link with Blake provides a connection for both Smith and Raine. It is the radical Blake who fascinated the critic/scholar in Raine (her biography of him attests to that) and it is Blake to whom the sketching, eccentric Smith, with her short, wrought poems has sometimes been compared.

Perhaps it is now, when with an attempt to take in the

enormity of Blake's work, to attend to it carefully, that we are also able to take in the sensibility and enormity of output of Smith and Raine, whose work and whose moment in history it is time to return to.

The words that took fire

Azita Ghahreman, *Negative of a Group Photograph,* tr. Maura Dooley & Elhum Shakerifar (Bloodaxe) £12

Reviewed by JAMIE OSBORN

Pushing into the losses that have accompanied her poetic career, Azita Ghahreman's is a voice of 'antique loneliness'. The poet's childhood as part of a land-owning family in Iran is a recurrent theme, while, in exile in Sweden, where she has lived since 2006, Ghahreman laments the loss of her language: 'I could not sing snow. / Oh for it to rain Farsi!' Maura Dooley's elegant, prosodically imaginative translations are filled with lacunae not in the Persian text, presumably to reflect the music and natural pauses of the Persian, but also suggestive of those moments when language can no longer directly express its source – a lyric tension as much as it is political. 'Glaucoma', for instance, figures post-revolution repression in Iran as a gradual blindness, and it is hard not to read an echo of an 'I' in the space between the words: 'The hollow of the eye   fills with snow', in Dooley's English.

Snow recurs as a metaphor of the chilling effect of loss, but the poet's passion equally flares to the opposite extreme of flame. 'Oh, the scent of your tender young blush', she writes in 'Freedom', 'the colour of the raspberries/you picked, red, a searing red/and the books the fire consumed –' The stink of burning books pervades the collection, as trauma, or a demon that creeps 'all the way up to Grandmother's stories', but fire is also a symbol of expression. In the title poem, memory is located 'Between the road that twisted around my neck / and the words that took fire in your mouth'. Occasionally the writing may seem sentimental, but in the best poems what the bridge translator Elhum Shakerifar calls 'the extremes of emotion', to which Ghahreman's Persian is given, blaze forth as defiant beauty, as in 'Prison', where 'like a welt from a whip / the trace of a kiss will remain.'

Despite, or partly because of, this headstrong quality in Ghahreman's voice, identity is a key and complex motif throughout the book. A poem titled simply 'Words' describes a woman variously as wind, flare, and veil, who 'slips into the scent of a lily', until she emerges 'in the shape of a woman who is nothing like her.' Poetry is her only home and protection as she crosses borders, yet in poetry, as Ghahreman writes in the 'I Unfolded the Earth', 'inner and outer worlds are at war, / in its language the river speaks deep and blue, / only

the word 'no' has a loving meaning.'

Poetry cannot be directed and is a source of both resistance and delight. In the gloriously funny 'Happy Valentine', in which the poet vigorously describes all the ways she will take revenge on a lover – a 'you' with 'gloopy eyes, like bowls of syrup, your stink of saffron and red roses, / your heart full of goodluck goldfish, wriggling up against each other' – the reader may ask whether the poet's true love is in fact her own irrepressible inventiveness.

Poetry takes many forms through the collection, flickering from exact visualisation to abstraction within a single line. Perhaps one of the most enduring metaphors is that of 'Spring', personified as a woman (significantly – as Shakerifar notes, Ghahreman's world 'feels distinctly matriarchal') returning to the desolation left by the Iran-Iraq war. With 'galloping clouds aflame at her heels' and 'death at her breast', the poem nevertheless ends with an image of patience and wonder that may speak for Ghahreman's practice, and for that of the translator:

she returns to use again
all that she unpicked from last year,
sewing, in every nook and cranny, in cerulean thread
the image of a bird –

pain, like a green stone, in place of its eyes,
and a wound where its mouth should be
so that it can sing out
its scarlet song.

Wanting to be

Mary Jean Chan, *Flèche* (Faber) £10.99; Chen Chen, *When I Grow Up I Want to Be a List of Further Possibilities* (Bloodaxe) £9.95; Alison Winch, *Darling, It's Me* (Penned in the Margins) £9.99

Reviewed by JONATHAN CATHERALL

With a debut collection as sure-footed as Mary Jean Chan's *Flèche,* I'm tempted towards the fencing metaphor which animates a finely balanced and pointed book. Such a temptation, however, is only a reflection of Chan's more profound strength: that she is one of those rare poets who leave you looking up with a sense that you can engage even the smallest part of the world around you with a much greater intensity. This is far more than the telling description which makes one see things afresh, though there are many of those. Intensity implies tension, and this book bristles with it, though its mesh is woven with great beauty and poise.

What's extraordinary is the fierce battle taking place between the poet and her mother, bout after bout of it, offence and defence, parry and riposte of anger and rejection and love on both sides. It is a battle which bleeds out into other relations: the ambivalence of a woman from Hong Kong writing in the English language, in the white world, in the straight world.

Tellingly, the book opens in the context of an exercise of authority which is also a reversal of it: the Cultural Revolution. The poet's mother relates dark fables drawn from this time, starting with adolescents slapping their teacher: 'their hands a stampede, their mouths deep trenches of bone'. We're invited to a scene of original trauma that has repercussions throughout the work, and in 'Conversation with Fantasy Mother', we see the attempt to compensate:

Dear fantasy mother thank you
for taking my coming out as calmly
as a pond accepts a stone
flung into its depths

The fantasy here figures a denial of the reality principle: the pond may 'accept' the stone, but we imagine the ripples. Chan is brave enough not only to air the family psychodrama, but to open up the question of the art work as itself an authority, or a form of denial. In 'Splitting', which embodies its title with two columns, her mother gifts a bed and plane tickets to her and her lover, but these become:

	missed items
the poet has now	singed so diligently
from the page	

With 'singed', Chan coopts a potential English language error – which might be made by any young child, but which resonates even more in the context of her ambivalent relation to English – to combine the act of singing and the act of burning. Poetry is figured simultaneously as the aestheticisation of a brand or wound, or compensation for it, or the razing of memory, or its raising 'from' the page into a song, as a form of memorial or burning resistance. Chan's work singes even as it sings.

With a title like *When I Grow Up I Want To Be A List Of Further Possibilities*, we know Chen Chen's busy and much-fêted debut is bound to steep us in excess and comic seduction. Other titles within the collection include 'Talking To God About Heaven from the Bed of a Heathen', 'Things Stuck In Other Things Where They Don't Belong', and 'For I Will Consider My Boyfriend Jeffrey' - this last after Christopher Smart, an affectingly cute encomium whose centrepiece is ten stages of Jeffrey observed shaving, and whose final stage might be a metaphor for the way Chen toys with his reader: 'For tenthly he holds back a giggle while I tickle the back of his neck with the buzzing razor.'

Painstaking Google research also confirms that, at 9" by 7", the book doesn't conform to standard or historic publishing sizes, although there is a range of classic exercise books in this shape. A wide octavo or a large foolscap quarto? With his expansive lines, Chen loves to inhabit the role of irrepressible schoolboy, or don his fool's cap – but although pink-orange jellyfish dance in azure on the cover of the book, prominent lines down its middle remind us that these are composite, constructed images; and suggest we are seeing the animals under glass.

At its best, Chen's work has a subversive sting. The designs which he exercises upon us are very conscious of his own dance. On the one hand, he's a camp, puppyish schoolboy with a desire for complete proximity to lovers and things in the world: 'I want to be a sweetheart in every moment,/full of goats and xylophones, as charming/as a hill with a small village on it.' ('Elegy For My Sadness')

In search of that closeness, the persona shifts to a poetic wide boy, a 'magpie', ducking and diving, happily putting his hands in and on 'things where they don't belong':

In this economy
of acute magpie syndrome. Where 'just a hobby' is the
strongest industry. & we work overtime at our reverie.
My weakness is loving this economy.
('In This Economy')

Though in a far hipper idiom, Chen reminds me of Mark Doty in his desire to embrace everything, to cover it with desire. At times, a frank and sensual passion for others, for bodies, and for objects in the world is, at least partially, freed from the ethics of suspicion and returned to a romantic craving for connection. However, as the book's cover-image suggests, central to the work is a recognition of postmodern mediation and distance, where even the angels are entirely lacking in direction:

God sent an angel. One of his least qualified, though. Fluent only in Lemme get back to you. The angel sounded like me, early twenties, unpaid interning. Proficient in fetching coffee, sending super vague emails.
('I'm Not A Religious Person But')

Self-regarding irony constantly mediates desire, though it doesn't remove it – if anything, it pushes it to a new, more alienated form. We could again compare Chen and Doty here, writing about the city. Doty recognises the role of the city in accelerating and multiplying desire, and appeals to a musical form, the 'deep house mix', to encompass it:

So much to want

in this city, the world's bounty
laid out, what's the point in owning

any one piece of it? Deep house mix:
('Mercy on Broadway')

With Doty, the metaphor is very turn-of-the-millenium: that of a track, bubbling with unreconciled tensions, but still to be loved and lost in. In Chen's poem, 'In the City', the metaphor appears initially to be a rather older one, in which the city, its bridges, its 'pork & chive dumplings we bought together', and the experience of being with the friend or lover eating the dumplings in Brooklyn, is likened to 'a feat of engineering'. Then something rather different happens. In a first phase, there's a figuring of the poet as weak and hollow, where being lost in the city is to crave its certainty and ambition and bow before it:

                    Tonight I cannot believe
the skyline because the skyline believes in me, forgives me
    my drooling astonishment over it & over the fact that this
    happens,
    this night, every night, its belief, glittering mad & megawatt
    like the dreams of parents.

This kind of 'drooling', loving abasement feels, as elsewhere in Chen's work, like a prelude to, but also a critical part of, the grandiose, hilarious flight that immediately follows:

                    By the way, is this soy sauce
reduced sodium? Do you know? Do we care? High, unabashed
    sodium intake!
Unabashed exclamation points!

Here, it feels that the metaphor of the city has transformed itself to that of a social media feed with its overactive exclamations. The knowing insignificance of the individual both produces, and gives way to, an ambition to perform himself and perform excess, in 'loving this economy'. This ambition is every bit as 'mad & megawatt' as the parental ambition, and later in the same poem Chen imagines himself atop the media industry:

                    Even here, in my fabulous
Tony-winning monologue of a New York, I'm struggling to get
    to the Joy, the Luck.

What feels equally significant is that the monologue is of 'a' New York. At one level, this is simply a reference to the personal story with its migrant inflections. However, it feels there's also a recognition that the monologue is partial, and no longer seeking to embody a unity like Doty's. This feels like a particularly twenty-first century dilemma. There's a refreshing honesty, a refusal to speak for everyone – but it goes hand in hand with a withdrawal from the public sphere into a splintered hall of mirrors, a route to 'winning' that ostensibly proceeds through self-deprecation, also recognised in 'Ode to My Envy' where 'My envy despises your more dramatic / & photogenic envy'.

Chen's sense of alienation, as a gay man and a Chinese American, is partly overcome by repeated acts of verbal ingenuity and heartfelt affection. But there are many poems and passages which directly face up to pain, as in the powerful 'Cuckoo Cry', in which his mother strikes him as a teenager for his 'beastly goo of wrong wanting', and in which:

Spring says it doesn't want to be personified,

wants to be forgotten. Doesn't want to be trigger
for memory.

Often, too, soft heart and sharp wit combine to brilliant and moving effect, as in these (mock-)Rilkean lines:

It seems the dead are busy with work we cannot

comprehend. & like parents, they don't want to tell you
what their jobs really consist of, how much they make.
    ('Elegy')

Alison Winch's dirty, clever, polyphonic debut *Darling, It's Me*, is preoccupied with sex, child birth, child rearing and more sex. Inner and outer interlocutors proliferate, from baby voices to portraits of Hobbes and Locke in dialogue as new mothers and 'real housewives'. Some voices carry a calm, teasing authority, whilst others scream with impotent rage and hormonal disquiet. In an early poem in the collection, 'Marriage', the husband's marriage:

    is a solid handshake.
Neighbours and exes covet it.

Mine is routine harassment; hung up
on uteruses
and training monogamy

A further voice wants to claw its way out:

The inner child of my marriage
is oral schizoid, masochistic,
prays for a defrocked rake

on a white horse
in all possible worlds.

Historical periods jostle into and out of anachronism. There's an extended rococo fantasia of eighteenth century sexual vagabondage with a marriage counselor, while 'Alisoun's' revisits a lushly horny Alison from Chaucer's 'Miller's Tale':

O love-lorn mourns at my loyns – *Nicholas!*

I want him down in this impish wood
its wayside shrynes / its dance of hazylnuts

However, the pastoral imaginings of the poem aren't tied to any constraint or diminution of female desire:

my cunt whystle-flutes
like crushable fowls
woo poppys & primeroles after morning rain–

Winch particularly delights in revisionist visions of major philosophers confronting the arse-end of their own systems of thought, bound in by sex and the body and childbirth: Spinoza 'lets go of his soft palate / for the salt leak of his cicisbeo's cock', while Hobbes 'wriggles on postpartum ring cushion' and 'hallucinates with sleep deprivation'. Berkeley, however, remains blithely apart in his idealisations: 'our dirt is done via carrier pigeons / born in the gin lanes of the historical metropolis'.

The cicisbeo – toyboy of a married, aristocratic woman – is a revealing figure. As in the Bakhtinian carnival, hierarchies are brought low, and inverted. There's a symbolic shaming and rendering absurd of all patriarchal pretensions, one in which men may be neutered or figures of fun or objects of carnal desire. In 'Daddy is Chilled', the poet runs the rule over a husband 'whose temples are military level squats ... whose armpits have a fat loss strategy' but who, despite the bathos of compulsive gym-going and male health obsessions, does seem to inspire a kind of lust and tenderness, his mouth 'rare but charred', his tongue 'quick-fire and tactical'.

Above all, Winch hauls up pleasure from the depths, welcoming the frank materiality of the body and the child's body, even in her literal and figurative chafing against it. As 'Expecting, the Gourd' puts it: 'This is your bed, now lie in it: ectopic pregnancies, / Bacchus, Pan, folic acid.'

Visionary

Jana Prikryl, *No Matter* (Tim Duggan Books) $15

Reviewed by EVAN JONES

In Jana Prikryl's poems – two healthy books of them now – there are very few questions. Announcements and pronouncements are delivered by a puckish, unemotional intelligence, a voice from the void, factual and often inconvenient. Her second collection, *No Matter*, is an expansive book, formally various and skillful. Her themes are the tragedy of our times: immigration, refuge, loss and change. It is poetry that seems practically stolen from the headlines. Twenty-four poems here share titles: 'Waves' (six), 'Anonymous' (seven), 'Friend' (five) and 'Sibyl' (six). This quartet is Prikryl's coat of arms, her shield, crest, supporters and motto. The repetitions direct our reading of the book, as the long-term friendships described break down, as an anonymous body found in the ocean is analysed for details. One 'Sibyl' begins:

> The officers wear plain clothes for weeks
> then unannounced for months will dress in uniform.
>
> I assume this is intended to keep me in
> suspense as to the nature of
> the structure of authority among them

The language is officious. The lines are taut, because the breaks are unexpected in insignificant places, so that the endwords have little weight. The sentence is pulled until it stops, ending by reinforcing, 'Suspense: / I've learned to let it hold me like a refuge.' The Sibyl seems more like Cassandra, the buzzwords of the internet era turned against her. In our age of photorecognition software, another 'Sibyl' ends:

> If they also accept resemblance
> as a phenomenon, you'll not
> be interned with anyone
> who doesn't speak your language

The various 'Waves' are the most loaded and considered. Their language draws on war and insurgency, the migrant crisis on the US-Mexico border, deaths in the Mediterranean, the climate out of control. The confusion

of these distinct issues in the poems is telling, and part of the calamity that Prikryl expands our understanding of. Everything is happening at once. Her waves batter the streets of Manhattan even as they appear to be elsewhere, turning an obstruction into an opening, in a language the newspapers recognise:

> At first so far from framing itself
> in waves it put a ceiling on itself
> at first, but every wall becomes a street
>
> Let it take so many generations, it will seem
> a street had been intended all along...

We understand the turns from place to place even as the incidents seem separate: Prikryl shows us they are one. The tragedy of young Alan Kurdi, the three-year-old whose body was found on the Turkish coast opposite the Greek island of Kos, photographed and circulated, continues to define the Mediterranean. It is hard not to think of him in another wave poem: 'No harm comes to him on that curving sand'.

Alan Kurdi is a reversal of Odysseus' arrival on the Phaikaian beach, and Prikryl calls that into question, via his recreation in the refugee Aeneas, wanderer of the Mediterranean and founder of an empire. Two poems draw out the connection, speaking across the book to each other, the sonnets 'Insta' and 'Epic', the titles reflective, both satirical in tone. The first begins:

> And do you suppose if there'd been phones that
> Dido would have chilled, monitored his posts
> as he sailed into a storm, the photos
> parading purple cumulonimbus...

While the second is more intimate and disturbing:

> [...] because the second night of his visit
> Dido begged a redo and he did it
>
> although if he glimpsed a new facet or
> felt shattered to relive it, or bored –
> her reaction tells us he said it
> just as he'd said it the night before.

Aeneas retells the story through books I–IV of the Aeneid, at Dido's request, of the fall of Troy and the details of his arrival in Carthage. Dido, fascinated, develops feelings of respect for him; the gods take the feelings further. Here, the themes of the poems come together, as they do in the best parts of *No Matter*. The subjects are serious, treated with intelligence and recognition, while the language is casual, 'chilled'. The patterns, we recognise, are the same, then and now, the irony of that sameness clear. Aeneas' 'redo' draws out ideas of PTSD in reliving his experiences, the soldier after the war, the refugee travelling over the sea.

Like Paul Muldoon, Prikryl juggles her themes and her vernacular in this way throughout the collection. But Muldoon pulls it all together, usually in a long poem, and that sense of cohesion is somewhat lost in *No Matter*, especially late in the book, which feels overstuffed. The memorial for Robert Silvers (1929–2017), editor of the

NYRB, a remarkable poem, when it appears is out of tune with the rest and doesn't fit with her grander criticisms. The same is true of the curious 'Bowie', a sort of dream-fantasy, perhaps, of a drive with a recently-deceased rockstar. If we are meant to read these two as we do the Aeneas poems, then 'Bowie' falls short, lacking the sensitivity of the stronger works. Or if they are connected to the 'Friend' series, then the poems suddenly become autobiographical in ways that aren't clear – why is David Bowie important here? The intimacies expand into more personal territory than elsewhere, perhaps (also like Muldoon).

Prikryl's *No Matter* is a visionary book, and while the vision doesn't feel entirely unified, there is a clarity that few poets are capable of.

Spellbinding Words

Robert Desnos, *A la Mystérieuse / Les Ténèbres*, translated by Martin Bell (Art Translated) £9.99

Reviewed by EDMUND PRESTWICH

Karl O'Hanlon's introduction tells us that these translations of the French Surrealist Robert Desnos were found in the papers of the poet Martin Bell after his death, and that they're published here for the first time. I'm no Surrealist aficionado but I'd strongly recommend this book, both for Desnos's own extraordinary imagination and for the beauty of Bell's English phrasing.

Writing that doesn't so much describe reality as create alternative realities of its own can seem spell-binding one moment and insubstantial the next. However, most of these poems do powerfully evoke the given world. For one thing, presenting familiar objects in bizarre contexts makes them strike our imaginations more vividly. On a larger scale, whole poems are constructed around collisions between fantasy and reality. And finally, of course, subjective feelings are themselves a reality of the world. In the poems that work – which I think is most of them – one feels convinced by the emotional development.

The collision between fantasy and reality gives its imaginative arc to 'The Voice of Robert Desnos'. Beginning softly, with ethereally intangible images – 'So much like flowers and breezes / like running water like fugitive shadows' – it rapidly escalates through a series of commands evoking the world-transforming magic of Shakespeare's Prospero or Ovid's Medea. Suddenly the poem shifts from aspiration to imagined achievement. For thirty five delirious lines the impossible is offered as actual, culminating in the cry, 'flesh quivers at my call.' Then everything shrivels into the desolate simplicity of negation:

the girl I love does not hear me
the girl I love does not understand me
the girl I love does not reply

So the poet's power seems useless if it cannot get him the one thing he truly wants. That's the reciprocation of his hopeless love for Yvonne George, the Belgian night-club singer who inspired these poems and who died of drink and drugs in 1930. A similar dialectic appears in more subtly interwoven ways in such haunting meditations as 'O Sorrows of Love!', 'I Have Dreamed Of You So Much', 'Never Another Than You' and perhaps above all 'No, Love Is Not Dead', with its intricate and astonishing shimmering of tones. Here, sad realism coexists with blazing erotic idealism. The reshaping of reality assumes a humbler form in the creation of a tender, protective voice enfolding George in the intimacy she denied in life. Humbling himself before George, though, Desnos declares himself fully the equal of Ronsard and Baudelaire simply because he knew and loved her.

Reading a translation that lives as poetry, you can't separate the work of the original poet and the translator. In single line after single line, Desnos brings ideas together with a mind-stretching strangeness that almost seems to constitute a miniature poem in itself – 'I bring you a little seaweed mixed with sea-foam and this comb', 'I struggle with fury against animals and bottles', 'the shadows of street-lamps and fire-alarms will make the night tired'. The precision with which such ideas strike the English reader's mind depends on the sureness of Bell's phrasing, the calm confidence of his cadences and the accuracy of his auditory imagination. He's created a style that transfuses French rhetoric and a French confidence in asserting abstractions into a distinctive but vital English. Perhaps the sensuousness of Desnos's own imagination acted as a bridge between the poetic traditions. And finally, Bell's translations of these poems have a remarkable rhythmic beauty that hovers between free verse and prose poetry: the integrity and precise weighting of each line is vital to their unfolding but sometimes a line is as long as a short paragraph.

Absence is Presence

Eileen Sheehan, *The Narrow Way of Souls* (Salmon Press) €12

Reviewed by DEIRDRE HINES

One of the most sacrosanct symbols in Irish poetry is, was but may not always be 'Mother Ireland'. The counter poetics that have been a hallmark of much recent Irish women's poetry have contested female representation as emblem, icon and cipher. Eileen Sheehan is an interpid waypaver in her reweaving and re-representing 'Mother Ireland' in 'The Narrow Way of Souls', her third collection and first to be published by the ever enterprising Salmon Press. Deaths in this collection abound: the two deaths of the poet's mother, the first from Alzheimer's , the next her physical passing, the death of mythologies and their rebirth in the relationship between this world and the world of the fey, and the death of grief after a journey that encompasses seven stages (shock, denial, guilt, bargaining, anger, depression and hope), and that is akin to a journey through the Underworld.

Sheehan presents her collection in fifty four poems encircled by seven haiku. Each haiku encompasses the theme and tone of the subsequent poems. The opening three poems introduce her thematic concerns and are not preceded by any haiku. She chooses to relive a favoured memory of her mother in the opening poem, 'The Greatest', reliving the boxing match between Mohammad Ali and George Foreman ' talking him up/talking him into winning. Her firm right hook/landing flush on the jaw/ of her own invisible opponent. ' And that invisible opponent takes tangible form in the following poem 'Alzheimer, C is for Carer'. Sheehan's last lines carry punches that carry a weighty aftermath. The tenderness that she suddenly feels for her ailing mother has come years too late, and the reader is reminded of Luce Irigaray's assertion that our culture is founded upon the matricide of the mother/lover. In such an alienating landscape, where the female is estranged from herself, it is little wonder that the fey beckon. The third poem in this opening sequence ,' The Stray' introduces the recurring motif of the power of faery and old traditions as a remedy against rational order that insists on women as less. If the stray is put on you, 'you'll walk forever in circles'.

Such confusion echoes some typical Alzheimers symptoms, and is a beautiful way of telling a truth slantly. Sheehan favours free verse in the majority of her poems, but there is an almost tanka like feel to many of her mostly four lined verses. The haiku that introduces the next four poems tells us that only the graveyard can be visited at home now. The poem ' Remedies ' relays a folk strategy for fooling death, and this bargaining forms the last verse of the poem.'For a person down the room on their deathbed/send for the wise one. She will screech Get out of my vision/at the first three creatures to pass by the door...' Death is fooled into taking these instead of the dying person.

The twelve poems in the next section address the many selves that comprise the identities of both mother and daughter. I loved the subversiveness of ' Sexing the Eggs ' in this section. The sex of each egg is determined by means of a wooden peg threaded with string. 'Clockwise circles marked an egg/as female, a straight line back and forth condemned/an egg as male.' Nature also serves as mother to the nascent poet, and as another reality to escape the crawthumpers in the poem of the same title, who ensnare every girl ' to expect nothing better '. There is a tradition of funeral poems told from the viewpoint of the mourners in old Irish poetry, and Sheehan reinvents this form with great humour in 'At Scartaglen Graveyard'. The poet and her sister are visited by a black cat as they visit family graves on a Halloween night. The final haiku encapsulates the journey taken through and under grief in three masterful lines:

Long road
the leaves and i
windblown.

Mother Ireland has been reinvented in this tour-de force that is as unforgettable as all our dead.

'the other way around'

Rowland Bagnall, *A Few Interiors* (Carcanet) £9.99

Reviewed by ANTHONY LAWRENCE

Prior to travelling in Ireland with my son, I bought books of poetry to sustain me during our weeks on the road. Among them was the Carcanet *New Poetries 7* anthology, which introduced me to a number of exciting new voices, with a highlight being the poetry of Rowland Bagnall. These poems proved to be the perfect road-trip companions as it rained almost every day, with fog so dense the landscape was all shifting shapes and shades.

The poems in his first book *A Few Interiors*, work like a series of entrances and exits in unmapped terrain with reduced visibility. The effect of navigating poems that often suggest rather than make implicit the details within a scene is, at first, unnerving, yet within a few pages the way to read these curious, luminous lines becomes evident. It's as though Bagnell has offered, early on, both caveat and explanation simultaneously: 'enter with caution, things may or may not be as they seem...'

There is a palpable sense of time being slowed to allow the narrator in many of these poems (Bagnall writes ' I like to think of these poems as having nothing to do with me personally, but get the feeling this is not the case') to isolate and explore objects within a physical or emotional landscape. Film is one vehicle for Bagnall's clever, paradoxical use of detachment as a means of locating intimacy. Take the second poem in Part One, *Viewpoint*, in which a scene from Hitchcock's *Rear Window* is aligned with the tension of watching a skydiver in freefall:

Alfred Hitchcock suddenly looks at us
through the glass frame of an apartment penthouse...

From up here I could see a skydiver looking backwards at a
    plane
as if it were falling away from him and not the other way
    around.

These lines go some way to defining the shape-shifting nature of Bagnall's gaze. One moment you feel you're on a safe, familiar footing, the next it's as though memory and imagination are unreliable witnesses and tour guides. This makes the poems more surrealist adventure board game than obstacle course, and they're often very funny.

There are a number of enduring themes and tropes that Bagnall uses cleverly: absence, illusion, height, distance and displacement, as well as references to painters, painting and film. On occasion he will push the boundaries of a word or phrase to breaking point, but he never oversteps the mark. This sense of being in control without foregrounding intention is one of the hallmarks of these poems, and it's part of what makes the work so remarkable.

Being self-referential can weigh a poem down with unnecessary attention on the poet, but when Bagnall takes us behind the scenes during composition, it only adds to the oddness and overall delight of his strange syntax:

> In the right context, *forever* can mean
> anything. Completely out of context, it means *space*.
> In my new notebook I write *drown*, then
> on a new line *balcony*.
>
> I picture my veins bursting like an over
> -pressured dam, pouring away, Old Testament red.
> In my new notebook I write *Old Testament red*, then
> on a new line *double doors*.
>   ('Hothouse')

This sleight-of-hand can be seen in many poems, especially those involving human interaction within the natural world, or in one of Bagnall's 'interiors' that have a disconcerting M.C. Escheresque atmosphere and design. In the title poem, time and distance are dovetailed with physical decay, and seen from the point of view of two people, in hiding, looking into a house:

> In the reflection
> there's a third person as well,
> but when I turn around they've gone
> which is a joke I've played on you before.
>   ('A Few Interiors')

Rowland Bagnall's mysterious poems call for repeated readings. His ability to combine, seamlessly, pop culture with raw human experience make this first book a compelling read.

The Old Soft Shoe

Leonard Cohen, *The Flame*
(Canongate) £22

Reviewed by DAVID C. WARD

The Flame is Leonard Cohen's last book in a long, productive and honoured career as a poet, singer/songwriter, performer and artist. He was assembling it when he died in 2018, aged 82, and it was completed by his son and two friends and colleagues. The book very much has the feel of a summation or a capstone of his career, consisting of three sections: final poems; lyrics to his last albums; and a hefty selection of entries from Cohen's creative notebooks. The volume is illustrated by Cohen's drawings, mostly full faced self portraits, sometimes accompanied by commentary and tag lines. Cohen's devoted fans, and they are legion, will want *The Flame* both as a final homage and on its merits.

Being in some sense a memorial volume doesn't make it, or Cohen's career, impervious to criticism, however. One of Cohen's hallmarks has always been an open vul-

nerability about masculinity and it's – or his – discontents: sex, work, failure, the uneasy roles of lover, husband, father, citizen. It's a style crafted in the mid 1960s as the older certainties and rigidities about masculinity crumbled under cultural changes ranging from the Civil Rights movement and feminism to the War and Vietnam and the popularization of soft drugs. I associate it especially with a university culture that favored introspection and self-analysis, sometimes to excess:

> Sometimes it gets so lonely
> I don't know what to do
> I'd trade my stash of boredom
> For a little hit or you

In the 1960s and '70s – and even now for all I know – you were always being told that you really had to listen to the words of a Cohen album; he was 'deep', not your usual rock'n'roll opportunist. To confess a bias, I always thought there was something a bit excessive, even opportunistic, about this stance of 'I'm vulnerable, me.' It can easily devolve into a mopiness or self-pity which actually is an evasion from (male) responsibility. It can be a pose, especially for men on the pull. This mopiness can be overcome in songs by the music which pushes against the lyrics (and to an extent submerges them; the dirty little secret about pop lyrics is they frequently make no sense) but which is hard to hide in the poems:

> the creature who says
> 'me' and 'mine'
> need not bend down in shame –
> along with lakes and mountains
> the ego is created
> and divine

Or the little poem 'My Career': 'So little to say / So urgent / to say it.' A confessional verse that doesn't admit guilt! It's no coincidence that the art work placed throughout *The Flame* is almost entirely self-portraits.

In bursts and jerks

Frederick Seidel, *Peaches Goes It Alone* (Faber) £10.99

Reviewed by IAN POPLE

Frederick Seidel has often divided critical opinion. On the one hand, the names of literary big-hitters populate the wrappers of Seidel's new book; Dan Chiasson, James Lasdun and Hanif Kureishi all offer puffs for Seidel's work. For such commentators, Seidel's sheer idiosyncrasy, chutzpah and unique voice give him a singular place in contemporary poetry. On the other hand, there are those, perhaps lower literary lights who find Seidel's parading of his own wealthy lifestyle and the endless name dropping insufferable. These commentators are likely to find his endless ironizing a kind of preening.

Seidel's career started in the shadow of Robert Lowell whose mannerisms and attack Seidel seemed to take on, lock, stock and barrel. And there are moments in *Peaches Goes It Alone*, where Lowell steps off the page. In 'Trump for President', Seidel reprises Lowell's 'For the Union Dead'; where Lowell has 'Behind their cage, / yellow dinosaur steamshovels were grunting / as they cropped up tons of mush and grass / to gouge their underworld garage', Seidel has '*Tyrannosaurus rex* on tires, gorging horribly, / Fucks the street in bursts and jerks.' Elsewhere it is Lowell's aping of Shakespeare's changing of word class. In 'Abusers', Seidel writes, 'Bring back that old-time Hollywood studio head – bring us his head! / His brutal bulk greenlights the groaning casting couch.' That 'greenlights' set amongst the alliteration seems straight out of Lowell, using the noun as a verb.

But these are anomalies in the general voice of Seidel's poetry; and it might be that he uses these gestures *because* the Lowell connection has been mentioned in other comments on his poetry. Another aspect of Lowell's poetry, which is carried over into Seidel's, is that sense of the patrician. With Lowell that sense was, perhaps, the feeling that Lowell was a deracinated member of that class. When Lowell wrote about his class, it was with a view to pointing up its limitations, in particular, with regards to its lack of political power. With Seidel, that sense of the patrician is ironized, although readers of his poetry might feel that irony itself is somewhat solipsistic. As noted before, part of the patrician in Seidel's poetry is the name-dropping. In this volume, we meet Mary-Kay Wilmers, editor of the *London Review of Books*, and the poet, Michael Hoffman. A whole poem arises from his friend, Dino Zevi's encounter with the pianist, Mauricio Pollini, in a lift at the Carlyle hotel, 'It is the week of the big art auctions in New York / And Dino Zevi, who has come over from London / for them leaves his room to do / What he's here for.' Elsewhere, Seidel has a tendency for 'product-placement'; many commentators have remarked on Seidel's clear love affair with Ducati motorcycles.

In part, Seidel 'gets away with' a lot of that kind of thing because the overall tone of the poems is genial and, to some extent, disarming. In addition, a Seidel poem is often not very linear. The reader may encounter one of Seidel's friends one moment but that encounter may quickly be replaced with something else. In the poem, 'Near the New Whitney', Seidel moves from remarking that a new maître d' is 'so gently lovely' to comments that 'There were violently drunkard painters downtown' who are now 'in the splendid new Whitney, dead / instead.', to beginning the following verse with 'I wished I had a sled dog's beautiful eye, / One blue, one brown, / To mush across the blizzard whiteout / Of sexy chirping chicks and well-trimmed / Bearded white young men. / You see how blue my old eyes aren't.' In 'To mush across the blizzard whiteout', Seidel shows that he has learned Lowell's gift for the precise description of the physical and the way it can be used as a metaphor; and also Lowell's gift for sliding that metaphor into a contrasting situation. These lines also show

Seidel's tone and style, in particular, the holding of the first person very closely to the empirical Frederick Seidel; the reader of this book would, by the end of it I suggest, have a very clear sense of the person that Seidel is. Across a whole book, that personality might feel just a little cloying.

Interrupted conversation

Thomas Goldpaugh and Jamie Callison (eds) *David Jones's 'The Grail Mass' and Other Works* (Bloomsbury) £130

Reviewed by HILARY DAVIES

It is forty-five years since the poet and artist, David Jones, died, and in that time his reputation has known the systole and diastole that those of many artists do after their death. For many years the recognition he received, or rather did not receive, seemed confirmation of the outmodedness of his way of life: Catholic in a time of relentless secularization, celibate and reclusive in the era of sexual liberation, an explorer of the sacred and incarnational nature of creation when everything around him shouted consumerism and materialism – an inveterate raider of the myth-kitty so famously disparaged by Larkin. All this helped to bolster an image of Jones as eremitic figure, pursuing obscure and old-fashioned, even obscurantist (in the root meaning of the term) interests. Not any more.

Such dismissal was, of course, always at odds with the fact that Jones' long poem, *In Parenthesis* is arguably the best poem of the First World War and was categorised by T.S. Eliot as a work of genius, while Auden called his second, *The Anathemata*, 'very probably the best long poem written in English this [twentieth] century'. This, coupled with Jones' achievements as an artist – he has been described also as the greatest watercolourist in Britain in the 1930s, and an engraver and calligrapher of great originality – makes him a force to be reckoned with by any standards. In recent years, this has indeed been acknowledged: an opera based on *In Parenthesis*, commissioned as part of the 1914–18 commemorations, premiered in the Welsh National Opera in 2016; a comprehensive retrospective of his art with accompanying monograph was put on at Pallant House in the same year; and there have been major television documentaries, conferences, and scholarly publications all devoted to reassessing Jones' importance.

'David Jones's *The Grail Mass and Other Works*' is one such. The editors explain their endeavour thus, 'what we have presented here is a composite text reconstructed from different sources' to try and piece together a version of what they have designated 'The Grail Mass', 'a separate work that should be judged on its own merit and not simply as a 'Rosetta stone' for the poet's later writings'.

This is a reference to the fact that from the late 1930s until he died in 1974, Jones was working on what he called 'fragments of an attempted writing', which is in fact the subtitle to *The Anathemata*, published in 1952. In his preface to this poem, Jones gives an indication of the difficulties that lie in the future for the editors of *The Grail Mass*, 'if it has a shape it is chiefly that it returns to its beginning. It has themes and a theme even if it wanders far. If it has a unity it is that what goes before conditions what comes after and *vice versa*. Rather as in a longish conversation between two friends, where one thing leads to another; but should a third party hear fragments of it, he might not know how the talk had passed from the cultivation of cabbages to Melchizedek... Though indeed he might guess'.

It is to this interrupted conversation that Goldpaugh and Callison seek to give some structure, or, at the very least, to 'restore Jones's work in progress'. The task is rendered more complex by the existence of *The Anathemata*, to which Jones *did* manage to give a coherent structure, and by that of two further collections, or compilations, from the same source, the volumes, *The Sleeping Lord* (1974), and *The Roman Quarry* (edited and published posthumously in 1981). This latter, to further confuse the issue, contains a fragment entitled 'The Grail Mass'.

That is only the start. Goldpaugh and Callison have had access to all Jones' papers and manuscripts, now housed in the National Library of Wales in Aberystwyth. It is a formidable archive. Jones was notoriously convoluted in his work, constantly revising, adding to and re-ordering it. René Hague and Harman Grisewood, Jones' close friends, were the first to attempt to organize the 1,300 sheets of unpublished material they found; they published this in the collections named above, and so much of the material the current editors are using has been previously publicly available. Goldpaugh and Callison admit that Jones' pagination of his manuscripts presents a 'dizzying array of numbers', and proceed to give an example which soon defeated this reader.

The way Jones' material is presented is also crucial to an appraisal. The editors have chosen to follow the poet's arrangement into 14 sections, which, they acknowledge, was done 'at an indeterminate stage in the compositional process'. This is a bit like trying to make something meaningful out of all Joyce's sketches for *Ulysses* (a work which much influenced Jones), including scenes he may not have wanted to use or felt ambivalent about, without the final version. Such attempts are most certainly not unworthy, but they are fraught with problems. Jones never did achieve the poetic 'Gesamtkunstwerk' he envisaged and tried over many years to write, which would have gone beyond The *Anathemata* and incorporated the texts of *The Sleeping Lord* and *The Roman Quarry;* and these publications may indeed only have seen the light of day because his friends cajoled and pushed him. Nevertheless, it seems rather to be wise after the fact to say that he 'blurred the original continuity' of his writing by moving to separate publication.

The Herculean task the editors set themselves, however, is not in doubt, and for this they must take much credit. In particular, by their fastidious editing, they point up the labyrinthine and mysterious process that is poetic composition. However, sticking to Jones' numbering and order does make it harder for the reader to discern swiftly which passages are completely new to publication. And that, after all, is what most Jones scholars will be interested in. It will also be mostly Jones scholars who will want to read this book, for the volume presupposes a level of knowledge of his published corpus that is extensive. Finally, the price tag of £130 places this edition firmly within the preserve of the university library. For those who wish to acquaint themselves with this most extraordinary of poets, the published editions of *In Parenthesis* and *The Anathemata* are the place to start.

Pointed and Proportioned

Cathy Galvin, *Walking the Coventry Ring Road with Lady Godiva* (Guillemot) £7; Christopher Reid, *Not Funny Any More* (Rack) £5; Andrew McCulloch, *The Lincolnshire Rising* (Melos) £5

Reviewed by RORY WATERMAN

I consider myself something of a poetry pamphlet anorak, but I can't define the format other than to say pamphlets are shorter than books, which doesn't mean much. Are the three tiny volumes on which Philip Larkin's reputation rests really pamphlets? No, they're not, though all are under the thirty-six-page limit for eligibility for the Michael Marks Awards for poetry pamphlets. Sometimes, what makes a pamphlet stick is a thematic unity, though we are now in an age in which themed full-length collections have also become normal in Britain – which probably often has something to do with the academisation of poets and the exigencies of the Research Excellence Framework. In any case, a thematic focus is still more commonly a trait of pamphlets, and it is what I am going to focus on here.

I often think of pamphlets as spineless wares, but that would exclude Cathy Galvin's beautifully-produced *Walking the Coventry Ring Road with Lady Godiva*, a numbered sequence, the subject of which you can probably work out. 180 lines of poetry are given a lot of page space here, as are Kristy Campbell's attractive and incongruously modern and abstract illustrations, though their relationship to the text isn't often clear. Nobody can know Coventry without knowing its terrifying ring road ('There are no circles of hell, just this road'), its vanquished car industry, the concrete legacy of its near-annihilation in the Second World War, and behind all of that, the figure of Lady Godiva, the speaker's companion in this set of ten poems. All of that is folded in here with the city of Galvin's youth, and its social and political tensions. In the opening section, the hooligans of Coventry City brush up against local punk heroes The Specials, in a nod to their 1981 hit 'Ghost Town' (itself a stark evocation of urban decay):

Beside me in the Cheylesmore underpass,
she took my hand and said: *Abandon fear.*
Sky Blues in red Doc Martens threw their cans

and punks in two-tone sang their ghost town near.
We walk to head to where an island framed
walls friars had rescued from a king.

Like Galvin, Philip Larkin grew up in Coventry; and unlike Galvin, he knew the city before, during and after the Blitz: 'In Larkin's shadow, I have drunk, too young, / in pubs surviving bombs', she writes. But, above all, this is a sequence in which the more giddyingly distant past is defined by the human detritus that hadn't yet overwhelmed it. In places, we might almost be reminded of *The Waste Land*, and Eliot's evocation of a pre-industrial River Thames that 'bears no empty bottles, sandwich papers, / Silk handkerchiefs, cardboard boxes, cigarette ends / Or other testimony of summer nights'. Here's Galvin, voicing Godiva (or 'Godgifu', the Old English variant the poet favours):

the river sinks beneath the streets,
holds its breath. Its secret stalagmites
hang where we hear the sigh,
whisper of years, echoes of prayer
bearing my name, Godgifu, to where
there is no rush of road, or tyres' febrile beat,
curve of tarmac, the world's passing.

Galvin can over-do it sometimes, repeating the same trick, and in places this pamphlet is a bit laboured and worthy. But she also packs quite a lot into these short pieces, and can be extremely evocative. A book-length equivalent, though? No thanks. This pamphlet stays about the full length of its welcome, unlike so many recent themed full-length collections.

And now let us move from one commanding figure to another, the President of the United States, who recently began a tweet by declaring his 'great and unmatched wisdom'. This is barely remarkable in our times, of course. The US has given the world a President nearly beyond parody – a figure who almost makes George W. Bush look restrained, and Barack Obama an impossibility. Christopher Reid's *Not Funny Any More* is a long, playfully-rhymed, loosely-metred poem about 'The Great Turnip', whose 'tweets are feats / of verbal facility', each 'a treasure / of wisdom compressed / into the best, / truest and smartest, / most genius opinions / you ever read'. It sometimes presents Turnip in a manner that might call to mind the previous president, were the irony not laid on so thick:

The Great Turnip
has all the qualities of leadership:
he is great, good, big, smart, excellent,
outstanding, and totally hip.

Charming as well,
plus cool and charismatic, he casts a spell
on all subgroups - male, female, whatever -
within his fan base or clientèle.

Reid's presentation of Turnip is often a little reminiscent of Roald Dahl's *Revolting Rhymes* – and it would all just be good, gruesome, childish fun were it simply make-believe:

Who is the enemy as of now?
The Great Turnip must decide.
He's feeling tough, he's feeling snide,
he needs an international row.

This isn't deep and meaningful stuff, though there is something intriguing about the way the title (spoken by Turnip as the last line of the poem) rings true across the whole text – not because it isn't a witty poem, but because it barely parodies the present dangerous and despicable reality. All the same, you won't learn a thing from this poetic portrait of vacuity – which, in places, seems to have been composed at something like the speed of a presidential tweet. That doesn't stop it from being entertaining. Again, more than a pamphlet of this sort of thing would just get on your nerves, after the joke wore thin.

Andrew McCulloch's *The Lincolnshire Rising* takes its title from an alternative name for the American Civil War, used by those who – like the current US President – regard the success of Lincoln's troops in that conflict as 'very sad and very bad'. Actually, it is named for an ill-fated rebellion against the dissolution of the monasteries and the establishment of the Church of England, which began when Louth Park Abbey in Lincolnshire was closed in October 1536, and ended conclusively a few months later with the execution of its leaders at Tyburn. These poems are not a sequence, but most are either explicitly or implicitly set in the poet's native county, specifically its hillier landscapes of the Lincolnshire Wolds, and adopt an historical or traditional focus. The first poem, also the title poem, is typically vivid and direct, not wasting time by explaining its circumstances, which are easy enough for the uninitiated to find out. Instead, the attention is on the intensity of apprehension:

Cromwell's men spread like a stubble fire
from field to field, threatening the houses.
A low sun gilds the trees. Its common wealth
burns in the furrows, sleeps in the clay.

Indeed, most of these are apprehensive poems – that is as much of a common thread here as the geography. 'October', a counterpart to the title poem, brings in another McCulloch staple, nature and seasonal change:

the crab looks dead already. Burst fruit
gape round its feet, bent nails scratch the sky.
The willow holds its breath, hardly dares move;
if once it shakes its head the game is up.

In 'Nightfall', dedicated to Tennyson (who, of course, was from the Wolds):

As silence spreads from coast to wold
And lights go out and hearths grow cold,
Earth falls still and voices cease
To leave the world awhile in peace.

This is even more cutesy and Georgian than the anthro-pomorphised crab apple and willow. But it also isn't, because once again, peace and security are on borrowed time, and the poem knows it. I'm not convinced all that many hearths go *hot* in 2019, even in rural Lincolnshire; the environments McCulloch depicts in this pamphlet are as traditional as his forms, without exception. But this suits his timeless subjects down to the apple-strewn, thorny, undulating ground. Yet again, this feels like an achieved pamphlet, the poems speaking to and through one another, the whole thing short enough for the connections to be remembered, and therefore more than the sum of its individual parts.

SOME CONTRIBUTORS

Sinéad Morrissey is the author of six collections, all published by Carcanet, and the recipient of both the T.S. Eliot Prize and the Forward Prize. She is Professor of Creative Writing at Newcastle University and Director of the Newcastle Centre for the Literary Arts. **M. Wynn Thomas** is Professor of English and Emyr Humphreys Professor of Welsh Writing in English, Swansea University. He is a Fellow of the British Academy and former Vice-President of the Learned Society of Wales. **Barry Wood** continues a commitment to MANCENT with recent courses on 'Cosmopolitan Sympathies: European WW1 Poetry' and 'Carol Ann Duffy: Testing Times'. The first course of 2020 is 'Poetry & Pollution: Prospects of a Silent Spring'. **Sarah White**, a former professor of French, lives, writes and paints in New York City. Her sixth collection, *Rock, Paper, and Broom*, is forthcoming from Deerbrook Editions. **Vahni Capildeo**'s new work, *Skin Can Hold* (Carcanet) and *Odyssey Calling* (Sad Press), written partly on Lindisfarne, exists thanks to a Douglas Caster Cultural Fellowship at the University of Leeds. **Sasha Dugdale**'s fifth collection *Welfare Handbook* is published by Carcanet in 2020. **Alex Wylie**'s debut collection, *Secular Games*, was published in 2018 by Eyewear. **Anthony Lawrence**'s most recent book of poems, *Headwaters*, won the 2017 Prime Ministers Literary Award for Poetry. **Hilary Davies** has published four collections of poetry from Enitharmon. She has won an Eric Gregory award, been a Hawthornden Fellow and Chairman of the Poetry Society of Great Britain. **Nina Bogin** lives in France. Her most recent collection is *Thousandfold* (Carcanet). **Annie Fan** reads law at Oxford. Their work appears in *Poetry London*, *The London Magazine* and *The Manchester Review*, among others. They are a shadow trustee at *MPT*. **Brian Morton** crofts and writes in the far west of Scotland, in sight of his ancestral Ireland. **Thomas Day** teaches English at Eton. He has published critical essays and reviews in *Essays in Criticism*, *The Cambridge Quarterly*, *PN Review*, the *TLS* and others, and has had poems published in *Agenda* and *English in Education*. **Brigit Pegeen Kelly** died 14 October 2016. Her family is currently engaged in the difficult task of determining what, of the work left behind, Brigit might have agreed to submit for publication. In that context, these two poems have been released. **Katherine Lockton** is co-editor at South Bank Poetry. She is featured in *Un Nuevo Sol*, a Latinx anthology. Her debut collection of poetry will be published with Flipped Eye in 2020. **John Fuller**'s long poem, *The Bone Flowers*, appeared in 2016; he has another collection coming from Chatto in 2020. His latest novel, *The Clock in the Forest*, was published in 2019. **Duncan Wu** is Raymond A. Wagner Professor of English at Georgetown University, Washington DC. He teaches people how to read poetry, but not how to write it. **Hugh Thomson** has written many books about travel and exploration, and won the inaugural Wainwright Prize for *The Green Road into the Trees*. He has given poetry readings at the Aldeburgh and Ledbury festivals. **Heather Treseler**'s chapbook *Parturition* (2020) won the Munster Literature Centre's 2019 chapbook prize. She is the Presidential Fellow for the Arts, Education, and Community at Worcester State University and a Visiting Scholar at the Brandeis Women's Studies Research Center.

COLOPHON

Editors
Michael Schmidt
Andrew Latimer

Editorial address
The Editors at the address on the right. Manuscripts cannot be returned unless accompanied by a stamped addressed envelope or international reply coupon.

Trade distributors
NBN International (orders)
10 Thornbury Road
Plymouth PL6 7PP, UK
orders@nbninternational.com

Design
Typeset by Andrew Latimer
    in Arnhem Pro

Represented by
Compass IPS Ltd
Great West House
Great West Road, Brentford
TW8 9DF, UK
sales@compassips.london

Copyright
© 2020 Poetry Nation Review
All rights reserved
ISBN 978-1-78410-830-4
ISSN 0144-7076

Subscriptions (6 issues)
INDIVIDUALS (print and digital): £39.50; abroad £49
INSTITUTIONS (print only): £76; abroad £90
INSTITUTIONS (digital): subscriptions from Exact Editions (https://shop.exacteditions.com/gb/pn-review)
to: *PN Review*, Alliance House, 30 Cross Street, Manchester M2 7AQ, UK

Supported by

Supported using public funding by
ARTS COUNCIL ENGLAND